AF711626

# SpringerBriefs in Computer Scienc

More information about this series at http://www.springer.com/series/10028

Kristof Kloeckner • John Davis
Nicholas C. Fuller • Giovanni Lanfranchi
Stefan Pappe • Amit Paradkar • Larisa Shwartz
Maheswaran Surendra • Dorothea Wiesmann

# Transforming the IT Services Lifecycle with AI Technologies

Springer

Kristof Kloeckner
Global Technology Services
IBM (United States)
Armonk, NY, USA

John Davis
Global Technology Services
IBM (United Kingdom)
Hursley, UK

Nicholas C. Fuller
IBM Research Division
IBM (United States)
Yorktown Heights, NY, USA

Giovanni Lanfranchi
Global Technology Services
IBM (United States)
Armonk, NY, USA

Stefan Pappe
Global Technology Services
IBM (Germany)
Mannheim, Baden-Württemberg, Germany

Amit Paradkar
IBM Research Division
IBM (United States)
Yorktown Heights, NY, USA

Larisa Shwartz
IBM Research Division
IBM (United States)
Yorktown Heights, NY, USA

Maheswaran Surendra
Global Technology Services
IBM (United States)
Yorktown Heights, NY, USA

Dorothea Wiesmann
IBM Research Division
Rüschlikon, Zürich, Switzerland

ISSN 2191-5768 ISSN 2191-5776 (electronic)
SpringerBriefs in Computer Science
ISBN 978-3-319-94047-2 ISBN 978-3-319-94048-9 (eBook)
https://doi.org/10.1007/978-3-319-94048-9

Library of Congress Control Number: 2018947830



This Springer imprint is published by the registered company Springer Nature Switzerland AG
The registered company address is: Gewerbestrasse 11, 6330 Cham, Switzerland

# Abstract

Today, the services industry is being disrupted by the digital transformation of their clients and of their own delivery processes. In this book, we will show how AI technologies can help to fundamentally transform the services delivery lifecycle to improve speed, quality and consistency. We will discuss how AI is applied to gain insight from operational data, augment the intelligence of experts and their communities and provide intuitive interfaces for self-service. While our use cases are taken from our practical experience of applying AI at scale in the IT services industry, we are convinced that these methodologies and technologies can be applied more broadly to other types of services.

# Contents

# Introduction

As more and more industries are experiencing digital disruption, using information technology to enable a competitive advantage becomes a critical success factor for all enterprises. Enterprises need to provide an engaging experience to their clients, while ensuring reliable fulfilment of the promised quality of service. In fact, their digital operations often determine the strength of their brand.

Faced with rapidly changing business needs and accelerating business cycles, enterprise technology leaders increasingly rely on a supply chain of services from multiple vendors. These leaders become service brokers and service providers to their lines of business. Like their own clients, they cannot and will not compromise between choice and reliability, and in their turn these leaders need the services they are using to evolve continuously. This provides unique opportunities for IT service providers to move from providing "piece parts" (fragmented service management support) and integrating systems to becoming services integrators themselves.

The ability to quickly adjust and expand services, to continuously improve service delivery based on operational insights, and to apply the knowledge of their expert teams become crucial differentiators for service providers. At the same time, growing complexity of IT environments like hybrid clouds, a deluge of data and high user expectations of instantaneous fulfilment of their service requests create significant challenges for IT service management.

This book describes a way forward from a service provider perspective; it will discuss the experience of the authors working for a leading technology services provider (IBM Global Technology Services), and the application of artificial intelligence technologies (which involve extracting knowledge, understanding structured and semi-structured information, reasoning, and learning) to the services lifecycle. The insights, technologies and methodologies presented apply broadly, to internal service providers and other industries beyond IT.



K. Kloeckner et al., *Transforming the IT Services Lifecycle with AI Technologies*, SpringerBriefs in Computer Science,
https://doi.org/10.1007/978-3-319-94048-9_1

## The Main Areas for Applying AI to the IT Service Lifecycle

For a service provider, there are three major problem spaces that hold promise for the application of artificial intelligence. We would, in fact, argue that they cannot be successfully addressed without also combining AI with automation and data analytics.

1. Gaining insight from operational data coming from hundreds of sources like event management systems, ticketing systems, incident root cause analysis, change logs, service requests and others and generated both by humans and systems. Service providers deal with thousands of client environments comprising millions of devices. They handle tens of millions of events per month and hundreds of thousands of change requests that contain both structured and unstructured information, making this a true big data problem.

   Insights from this data need to be made actionable. This can lead to preventive actions to remove the causes of situations, and thus improve the quality of service overall. Operational data can also be used to **automate the responses even to non-deterministic use cases, or at least to provide input for better human decision making**. Machine learning is indispensable for this problem space, but approaches taken in other domains have to be adapted to the unique circumstances of IT, as we will demonstrate in later chapters.

2. **Capturing and enhancing expert knowledge throughout the lifecycle.** Very few individual experts have all the knowledge required for complex environments spanning hybrid clouds and infrastructure and applications from many different providers. Knowledge is often spread across many internal and external sources. Sometimes the most important organizational knowledge is tacit, rather than explicit. Artificial intelligence technologies like concept extraction, text understanding and mapping to domain ontologies can help to apply the right knowledge consistently and in a timely fashion, whether it is during solution design, operational health checks or compliance control. AI-infused tools would in most instances serve as advisors or virtual 'buddies' to human experts.
3. **Enabling self-service** for service requests and problem resolution, through intuitive natural language interfaces. The main AI challenge here is to correctly identify the user's intent and to map it to an automated resolution in most cases, and in the remaining cases give services personnel additional information to improve speed and quality of the response. Over time, these approaches can also deliver a more personalized experience through learning about the users and their context.

In our experience, where enterprises have invested in automation, but the results do not meet expectations, this is usually due to insufficient attention to the value of data. By using analytics enhanced by AI enterprises can remove systemic issues within the environment, instead of automating a reaction to unsolved problems.

They can also arrive at fact based prioritization of automation targets. By adding AI to enhance automation, a larger set of use cases can be addressed, where previously humans would have had to be involved to complete tasks.

## Transforming the IT Services Lifecycle into a System of AI-Supported Feedback Loops

In our experience, applying AI to the three areas described above will profoundly transform IT service management. Using a simple analogy from biology, AI provides the brain (insights) and automation serves as the muscle (action). Information about the systems under management is constantly **fed back** into the 'brain', augmenting the knowledge base, and enabling further learning to produce better outcomes.

Through these feedback loops, systems begin to understand, reason and learn and thus become self-healing and self-optimizing. In other words, we are finally beginning to realize the vision of **autonomic systems**.

The IT services lifecycle operates on three levels (or in three domains) as show in Fig. 1:

1. Designing and building superior IT solutions **(Solution Design or 'Design' Domain)**
2. Managing IT operations to keep the environment healthy and 'always on' **(Services Management or 'Manage' Domain)**
3. Optimizing IT performance for better business outcomes **(Services Optimization or 'Optimize' Domain)**

**Each of these levels constitutes a feedback loop**, as data is captured and analyzed and knowledge bases are enhanced and refined. Looking at this from the inside out (from operations to optimization to design) moves us from an immediate to a longer-term horizon and increasingly towards business contexts. These domains are interconnected, for instance data gathered during operations (the manage domain) will point to improvement potential and even better designs.

To make sure these connections are actually established and to avoid fragmentation into a multitude of disparate 'AI projects', it is extremely important to take a

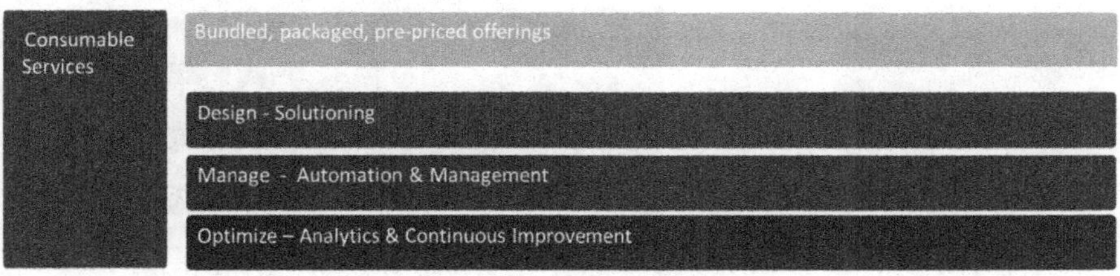


**Fig. 1** IT services lifecycle domains

systematic approach across all three domains with a common data lake, common ontologies and knowledge bases and a comprehensive set of consumable services, including artificial intelligence and automation. Ultimately this will establish an **AI platform for services management.**

In the following paragraphs we are going to describe an example of such a platform referred to as the **IBM Services Platform with Watson or The Platform**, and later we will discuss the properties of such platforms in more general terms. The main elements, as described in Fig. 2 are organized around the three domains (Solution Design, Services Management, Services Optimization) discussed above.

The foundation of the Platform is data, a Data Lake comprising of data stores for both short-term and long-term information gathered running IT infrastructures across more than 1200 accounts and 120 different data sources, like tickets, service requests, root cause analysis reports etc.

This data is used by the content of the Optimize layer of the Platform. The Optimize Domain operates through the lifecycle of a given system and focuses on generating cognitive insights from a larger context of data drawn from all accounts on The Platform and driving proactive actions for increased system health and delivery quality. A wide collection of analytical techniques, augmented with AI technologies. This is the underpinning of Cognitive Delivery Insights, using AI technologies like text analytics, entity extraction, or retrieve & rank available as IBM Watson cloud services [1], as well as machine learning technologies directly developed in a cooperation between the technology services and research teams. The system currently has tens of pre-built insights and supports account specific dashboards. AI enhanced analytics draws on subject matter expertise in support of use cases like continuous technical health check (deployed in 60 accounts), predictive analytics for server incident reduction (deployed in more than 100 accounts), change risk assessments and faster root cause analysis. Chapter "Gaining insight from operational data for service optimization" provides further details for this domain.

The Manage Domain contains a broad and deep set of automation capabilities ranging from Robotic Process Automation (RPA) to in-line transaction automation. The ambition for which, when extended with AI is to automate everything we do. In the server management space analytics insights are used to pre-emptively remove the causes of incidents, with the remainder either being fully remediated or assisted

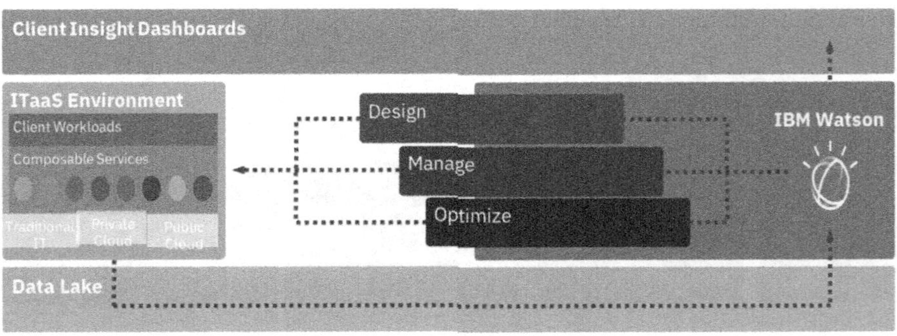


**Fig. 2** IBM services platform with Watson

by automation. Dynamic Automation uses event management to filter out events that do not require action, uses machine learning to classify tickets, and auto-resolves actionable tickets for which automations have already been written. At more than 1000 accounts, analytics including Watson technologies is used to fine-tune automation approaches. Moving all accounts to the best of breed allows to continually improve automation yield, now automatically resolving or assisting the resolution of more than 75% of all tickets handled by incident automation. For auto-resolved tickets, an average reduction of mean time to recovery is 90%. By continuously enriching these technologies, the system can perform more and more analysis in real time, as opposed to offline. A detailed description of AI technologies used in Manage Domain is described in the following chapter "Gaining insight from operational data for automated responses".

The platform is also addressing digital labor and using AI technologies for help desk and assistance tasks. Technology support services use agent assist technology with a great success. Workplace Support Services powered by Watson is an end user assist capability able to directly discover end user intent and to provide self-service help through conversational interfaces. More details could be found in the chapter "Conversational IT Service Management".

The Design Domain operates with the longest time horizon. Cognitive technologies are used here to capture and manage organizational knowledge and provide best practices guidance throughout the delivery lifecycle, starting with solution design. The Platform provides IT as a Service as well as standardized composable offerings, reusable solution building blocks and patterns. The current challenge is in picking the best solution using existing building blocks and experience from engagements to advise on the best solution for a given customer service request. This will augment the prescriptive guidance on how to set up hybrid clouds. The goal is to build a suite of cognitive tools targeted towards Technical Solution Architects and Managers to enable them to quickly extract functional and nonfunctional requirements from Request for Proposal (RFP) or Request for Service (RFS) documents and map them to solution building blocks as a basis for rapid co-creation of solutions together with clients. The knowledge underpinning these tools is being sourced both from existing solution and offering artifacts as well as from curated social content contributed by our expert community. For more information, see chapter "AI for Solution Design".

Finally account specific dashboards allow immediate visibility and drill-down into problems affecting services performance and availability by presenting information from the solutions in the three design, manage and optimize domains. This enhanced level of visibility allows accounts and clients to drive targeted 'get to green' actions..

As already stated above, all three domains are designed to feed into each other. Underlying (federated) ontologies provide the 'glue' between the different levels of cognitive insights and enable micro and macro learning mechanisms supporting each other. For instance, learning that does not yet lead to automatic actions can still feed into the corpus of knowledge aiding a human expert.

The following table describes the profound transformation of specific aspects of IT services management through AI in a 'before/after' view (Table 1).

**Table 1** 'Before/after' the transformation of specific aspects of IT services management through AI

| Before | Example | Result | After | Example | Result |
|---|---|---|---|---|---|
| *Deterministic* | Dynamic automation receives events and matches them directly with automations to resolve. | Events which have more than one potential resolution can't be fixed by automation. | *Non-deterministic* | Dynamic automation identifies event patterns, runs associated diagnostics and then executes automations to address the root cause. | Events with multiple causes and multiple potential remediations can be remediated. |
| *Structured* | Robotic process automation can only process structured input. | Service catalogues and forms are needed to direct behavior. | *Unstructured* | The meaning of unstructured mails, tickets, chat conversations can be extracted and used to direct automation. | Increased volume of use cases that can be addressed without human intervention. |
| *Manual* | Requirements and baselines are identified manually from customer requests. | Days spent that could be better used engaged in collaborative client dialogue. | *Automatic* | Requirements and baselines are automatically extracted in minutes. | Allows for co-creation process with client (i.e. fast confirmation of needs and subsequent tuning) enabling high quality solutions tailored to business requirements. |
| *Limited by current experience and status quo* | Change risk ratings based on experience and estimation. | Incorrect assessments leading to over and under management of changes, resulting in incidents as a result of change. | *Statistically proven* | Change and incident analysis with natural language processing, provides predictive change risk analysis based on historical fact. | Increased accuracy of change risk analysis resulting in fewer incidents as a result of change. |

(continued)

**Table 1** (continued)

| Before | Example | Result | After | Example | Result |
|---|---|---|---|---|---|
| *Technical queries & navigation* | Structured database queries to extract information. Navigation through visualization of data. | Harder than it needs to be, as you need to know what you are looking for and how to get to it. | *Conversation* | Natural language discussion that in the background formulates and collects the required information. | Quicker more intuitive access to answers. |
| *Individual knowledge & investigation* | Information is used from many sources of knowledge from ticket history to knowledge repositories, but its not possible to distil a single source of truth. | Slow and limited discovery of information. Answers are based on the best that can be found. | *Vast knowledge corpuses intelligently mined* | Curated knowledge on many subject domains, enhanced by experience and results; accessed via a conversation. | Quick resolution to the best answers. The best answers available. |
| *Compliant with the potential for some hidden causes* | Continuous compliance delivers compliance dashboard and corrects non-compliant situations daily, however deep insight into systemic repeating issues is difficult to derive from the masses of data. | Some underlying causes of non-compliance are not identified and addressed. | *Compliant with complete transparency* | By introducing AI to analyse the data and identify patterns, it is possible to highlight anomalies that require further investigation | Underlying root causes of non-compliance are identified and they can be addressed via action plans. |
| *Manual* | Requirements and baselines are identified manually from client requirements, federal and industry regulations and vendors security guidelines | 6–9 months are spent analyzing the security requirements and merging the requirements into a consolidated document. | *Automated (ML)* | Requirements are extracted in minutes, and merged with multiple regulatory items for validation with an expert to identify the control points for automation. | Fast identification of applicable policies to each situation, accelerating the implementation of controls. |

(continued)

Table 1 (continued)

| Before | Example | Result | After | Example | Result |
|---|---|---|---|---|---|
| *Limited coverage of automation No information support to drive proactive decision to be compliant* | No visibility on risks or vulnerabilities caused by applying or deferring patches | Patch deployments to address vulnerabilities are continuously deferred. | *Automated (ML, AI planning, knowledge discovery)* | AI based risk models that simulate the results of applying or deferring patches. These inform the patch management solution and what is placed within the fixed patch windows, providing evidence based prioritization. | End to end automation for patch deployment at workload level. Client infrastructures are more safeguarded with less vulnerabilities. |

## Core Elements of an AI Platform for the Services Lifecycle

In the prior segments, we have already discussed some elements of AI-driven platforms for the services lifecycle, with an example of the IBM Services Platform with Watson implemented by the authors. We now look in more detail at the general structure of such platforms. For the purposes of our discussion, we distinguish three main constituent parts (Fig. 3):

1. **Consumable services** pertaining to the lifecycle domains referred to as 'Design, Manage, Optimize' in Fig. 1, directly interacting with the managed environments
2. **Common content** like the Data Lake
3. **Common services** that are reused by other consumable services, including AI features.

### *Consumable Services*

A Platform serves to deliver content to its users. In the IT Services domain such content would generally include systems management, automation, dashboard, reporting and analytics solutions. We call content of this type "Consumable Services".

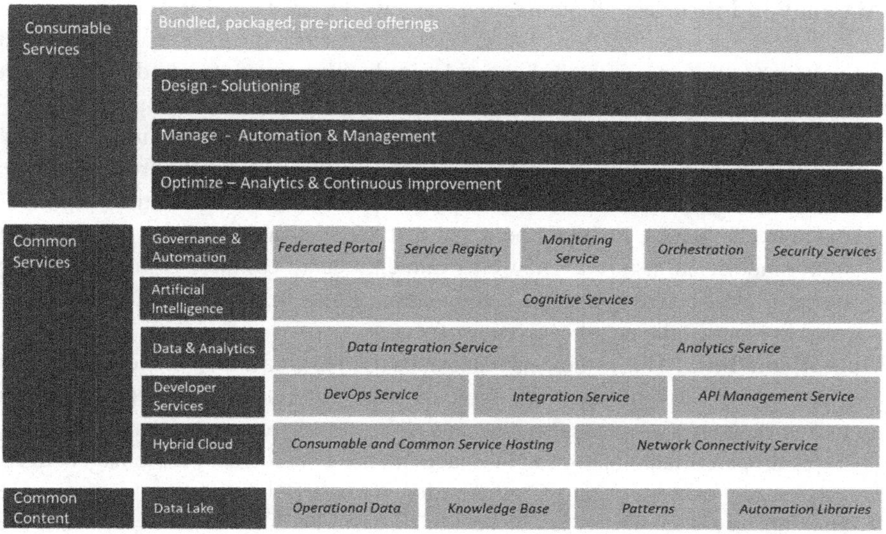


**Fig. 3** IBM services platform with Watson for service lifecycle

They are consumable by IT support and management teams, as well as other management applications (through APIs) and are used to design, manage and optimize enterprise IT environments, as described in the example of the IBM Services Platform with Watson. The following chapters of this book will describe in more detail how AI infuses these domains.

## *Common Content and Data*

We believe that data and the insight provided through analytics and artificial intelligence is key to continuous service improvement. In our experience, the implementation of automation solutions alone will usually fall short of expectations without an intense focus on the creation of common content and the consistent use of data to understand systemic issues and gain recommendations on how to improve outcomes.

Common Content includes:

**Knowledge** in architected knowledge bases and their ontologies, accessible through APIs, but also artefacts like the content of run books or live chat dialogues facilitated by AI conversation engines.

**Patterns** are used throughout the lifecycle and embody best practices and standards.

**Automation Libraries:** all automation frameworks need content to operate, open or framework specific automations, robots, scripts. Having a library of predefined content for the applications that reside on the platform not only delivers a fast start with quicker time to value after implementing automation, but also it benefits from having been tried and tested in other situations. We find that when connecting new environments to the platform, they all benefit from the same initial set of reusable content as they all experience the same underlying automatable challenges. It should be noted that even reusable libraries usually need minor modifications in each new environment, regardless there is value in having reusable intellectual capital as a foundation. From that point, analytics can be used to identify the next best area for focus.

**Operational Data:** This is the data that can be used to create information and action plans to improve outcomes. The more data the better, insight is created by comparing outcomes associated with many different sets of content and outcomes. Typical operational data in the IT space includes, incidents, problems, changes, service requests, asset and Configuration Item (CI) information, performance and capacity data. The types of insight that can be derived is covered in more detail within the next section. As well as analytics driven insights, the amassed historical data is also used to train artificial intelligence engines and may be used in combination with automation.

We highly recommend creating a data lake for the operational data as a better approach than data warehouses, given the evolving needs to combine data from heterogeneous and changing data sources.

## *Common Services*

Common Services support Consumable Services to fulfil their objectives. A solid platform will have three types of Common Service:

1. **Hosting & Management**: these common services provide the actual physical hosting of the consumable services in data centers. They provide the necessary physical and logical environments in which to host consumable services. These are usually distributed into multiple geographies in line with IT service customer wants and needs and data movement considerations. Notwithstanding they will be deployed using a standardized hosting model. Virtualization is standard including software defined networks to deliver maximum agility when deploying consumable services for customers.

   While consumable services are used to "manage" customer's IT, run their business applications and even automate their business processes, they too need managing. Any failures in consumable service operations, especially where automation is involved would render essential work undone. Additionally, as these systems will invariably have access to customer's business critical applications security management also must be considered.

Finally, there is a need for secure methods of connecting the Consumable Services to the environments being managed, so secure network is needed.
In summary, having Hosting, Management, Security and Network Connectivity Common Services are all important attributes of a Platform. The consolidation of consumable services and their management leads to increase speed of deployment, and increased service quality for service providers adopting a Platform based approach.

2. **Development, Deployment and Execution**: customers expect continuous innovation, when signing multi-year contracts, it is rightly expected that the technical solution being used to manage the clients Enterprise will evolve, continuing to both reduction in services costs and increase in quality of the services. As a result, it is important that the Platform supports this continued evolution with a DevOps pipeline. Existing solutions can continue to be evolved, and new ones could be easily implemented to the hosting point of presence that has been established for each customer using the Hosting and Management Common Services.

   In IBM, for example, this allows the quick deployment of innovation from IBM Research to the "managing" environments quickly. The platform resolves non-functional challenges that would otherwise exist around security, backup, monitoring, which could cause adoption lag, while allowing Research to focus on the differentiating core functions. Typical Common Services in this Domain would include DevOps pipelines, Orchestration, containerisation, integration and API services to make the connectivity between Consumable Services easier to achieve.
   The presentation of consumable services would optimally be handled via a persona-controlled portal allowing users of consumable services to gain access to them, via single sign on, but also have the opportunity via a catalog to view services they don't currently have and request they be provisioned. Common services would handle the automated execution of this, and then access is provided back via the portal.

3. **Usage**: the final set of common services are associated with consumable service execution. These are common services that provide functionality that multiple consumable services can take advantage of. This would include core AI services, some of which may be provided by vendor cloud services.

## Establishing an AI-based Innovation Eco-System

If the platform is sufficiently open and has Common Services that provide value, then a developer ecosystem can be established around it. A developer ecosystem allows third parties to develop content, Consumable Services that utilize Platform Common Services. It is also possible for new Common Services to be provided by platform ecosystem developers.

The advantage for third parties is a wider audience for their solutions and new revenue streams, while customers (users) of the platform get increased functionality.

Customers can also get involved in the Platform developer eco-system, by being taking part in pilots or sponsoring the development of Consumable or Common Services. As an illustration, a customer could identify the need for a new solution, and may choose to fund its development for their own usage. They would participate by shaping the user stories and contribute to sprint play backs. Because of their contribution, they could expect to receive royalties based on the usage of the Consumable or Common Service with other customers. This model allows any enterprise in any industry to diversify into IT development beyond their core business.

For an ecosystem to operate effectively there needs to be high quality intellectual capital describing how to develop against the platform, so that content providers may be as self-sufficient as possible. During its infancy this could be coupled with a platform ecosystem support organisation, so that expertise is available to assist. During this early period, partnerships would tend to be managed. In a fully mature model, eco-system participation would be fully open, along with the existing intellectual capital, queries would tend to be resolved via social media and crowd sourcing solutions. We believe that any platform encouraging eco-system development needs to have the following capabilities

- The ability to ingest data from any source and deposit it into a data lake, with a published API
- A pluggable framework for AI technologies
- Data analytics and visualization technologies that allow for self-service
- A federation mechanism for pluggable knowledge-bases with underlying expandable ontologies
- A mechanism for social curation of knowledge bases

These capabilities create a basis and an incentive for teams to use the platform for innovation, leading to acceleration through reuse. However, technology is just a starting point, significant changes in culture and process are also required. The following elements are essential for success:

- A systematic approach to capturing and maintaining organizational knowledge that becomes engrained in the culture and processes and addresses the entire lifecycle of knowledge.
- A strong knowledge community with a technical leadership that acts as stewards of the knowledge lifecycle
- Rewards, role models and executive commitment to foster a culture of knowledge sharing and social curation of knowledge
- Strong metrics that demonstrate the business value of investment in the knowledge lifecycle

The cultural and organizational elements described above can be reinforced by platform-based tools that deliver immediate value to practitioners, like advisor tools that allow an individual to tap into the collective knowledge of the community and experience the value of shared knowledge, while at the same contributing back additional knowledge and experience. This ultimately leads to an agile approach to development of these tools and the supporting knowledge bases.

Making the expert community the stewards of an AI-based service lifecycle will greatly reduce resistance and lead to faster adoption.

## Overview of the Content of the Book

We will conclude this introduction to AI technologies for IT service management by giving a brief overview of the application of AI to automated incident responses, service optimization, recommender systems for IT solutions and conversational self-service systems. In all cases, the nature of the problems we are addressing and the shape of the data available to us made it necessary to devise novel approaches by adapting strategies from other domains like healthcare and blending technologies in unique ways.

### *Gaining Insight from Operational Data for Automated Responses*

We focus our discussion on applying AI to the automated resolution of incident tickets, and the methodology and technologies for analyzing tickets, eliminating those that don't require action as well as auto-resolving those that do. This relies on novel domain specific techniques in data mining and machine learning to generate insights from operational context, among them generation of predictive rules, deep neural ranking and hierarchical multi-armed bandit algorithms. New capabilities improve the quality of services provided to customers, drive enhanced yield for automated event and incident resolution, and offer an increased operational visibility for clients and service providers alike.

### *Gaining Insight from Operational Data for Services Optimization*

We discuss ticket analysis with the aim of identifying further opportunities for automation and to achieve best of breed results by comparison across multiple installations. We again focus on aspects of 'understanding' ticket content like dealing with 'noisy' information, ticket vectorization and canonical correlation analysis. This approach has been widely deployed within IBM and has led to significant service improvements.

We also look at how to reduce the risk of service disruption from failed change by predicting problematic changes.

## *AI for IT Solution Design*

Cognitive Solution Designer supports technical solution managers and architects to process client requirements, prepare sound technical solutions, and respond to client service requests and RFPs in a timely and effective manner, significantly reducing a previous multi-month process. Attention is given to the end-to-end user experience. As next natural evolution, the solution will eventually an RFP (or an RFS) response and produce contractual work products.

## *AI for Conversational Self-service Systems*

Increasingly, chatbots are becoming an interface to services in the personal realm. We discuss the unique challenges for providing conversational interfaces for expert users to get precise and helpful answers to domain specific questions, in particular for guided troubleshooting. We are also looking at how to address the challenge of scalability of subject matter involvement.

## Conclusion

In this book, we are presenting core areas for the application of AI to IT service management: Gaining insight from operational data and driving automation, augmenting expert knowledge throughout the knowledge lifecycle and enabling end-user self-service through conversational interfaces. Together they enable a paradigm shift in IT service delivery ushering in the era of technology-run/services integration. The authors have implemented the solutions discussed in this book in the context of the IBM Services Platform with Watson, which has been widely deployed in IBM Global Technology Services with positive impact on service delivery quality.

We are addressing both IT practitioner and research audiences by discussing implementation strategies and areas for further research to address the unique challenges of IT with a combination of complex and heterogeneous systems and extremely noisy data.

We believe that given the growing the growing complexity of IT environments coupled with the increased demands on their availability and performance AI holds the key to success through the entire IT services lifecycle.

## References

1. Kloeckner K et al Building a cognitive platform for the managed IT services lifecycle. IBM Res Dev 62(1). Available https://ieeexplore.ieee.org/document/8269344/authors?ctx=authors
2. https://www.ibm.com/cloud/

# Gaining Insight from Operational Data for Automated Responses

## Background

Facilitating autonomic behavior is largely achieved by automating routine maintenance procedures, including problem detection, determination and resolution. System monitoring provides effective means for problem detection. Coupled with automated ticket creation, it ensures that a degradation of the vital signs, defined by acceptable thresholds or known patterns, is flagged as a problem candidate. It is a known practice to define thresholds or conditions that are conservative in nature, thus erring on the side of caution. This practice leads to a large number of tickets that require no action (false positives). Elimination of false positive alerts is imperative for effective delivery of IT Services. It is also critical for the subsequent problem determination and resolution. All operational data, including events and problem records, will be used for automated resolution recommendation.

A typical workflow of ITSM is illustrated in Fig. 1. It usually includes six steps: (1) As an anomaly is detected, an event is generated and the monitoring system emits the event if it persists beyond a predefined duration. (2) Events from an entire IT environment are consolidated in an enterprise event management system, which upon results of quick analysis determines whether to create an alert and subsequently an incident ticket. (3) A monitoring ticket is identified by IT automation services for potential automation (i.e., scripted resolution) based on the ticket description. In case the issue could not be completely resolved, this ticket is then escalated to human engineers. (4) Tickets are collected by an IPC (Incident, Problem, and Change) system. (5) In order to improve the performance of IT automation services and reduce human efforts for escalated tickets, the workflow incorporates an enrichment engine that uses data mining techniques (e.g., classification and clustering) for continuous enhancement of IT automation services. Additionally, the information is added to a knowledge base, which is used by the IT automation services as well as in resolution recommendation for tickets escalated to a human.

 
K. Kloeckner et al., *Transforming the IT Services Lifecycle with AI Technologies*, SpringerBriefs in Computer Science,
https://doi.org/10.1007/978-3-319-94048-9_2

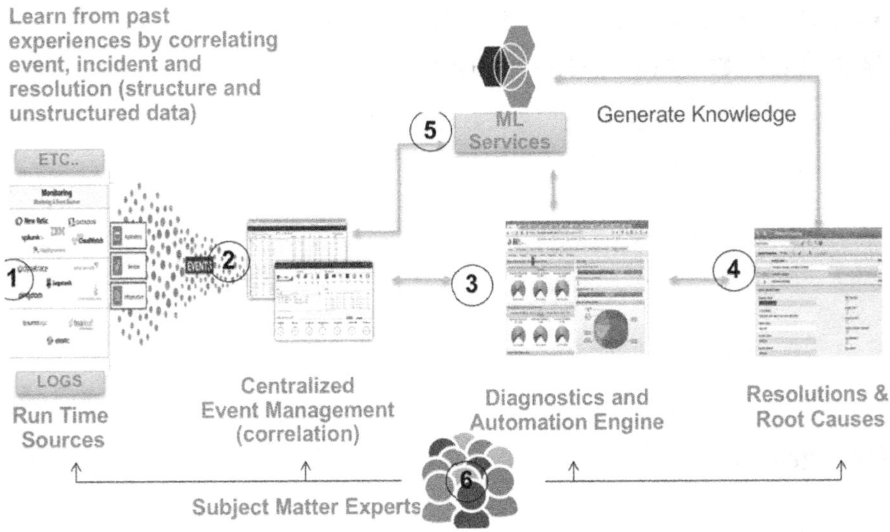


**Fig. 1** The overview of ITSM workflow

(6) Manually created and escalated tickets are forwarded to human engineers for problem determination, diagnosis, and resolution, which is a very labor-intensive process.

## Eliminating Non-actionable Tickets

The approach we discuss in this chapter targets eliminating false positives at the time of transformation of the detected-problem candidate into an open ticket. The goal is to reduce the number of non-actionable tickets generated from monitoring alerts, while all actionable tickets are retained. This is achieved by deriving optimal monitoring conditions and alert delays through the analysis of historical alerts and tickets.

### *Challenges*

Our goal is to refine original monitoring situations, eliminating as many non-actionable alerts as possible while retaining all real alerts. A naive solution is to build a predictive classifier into the monitoring system. Unfortunately, no prediction approach can guarantee 100% success for real alerts, and even a single missed one may cause a serious problem, such as a system crash or loss of data.

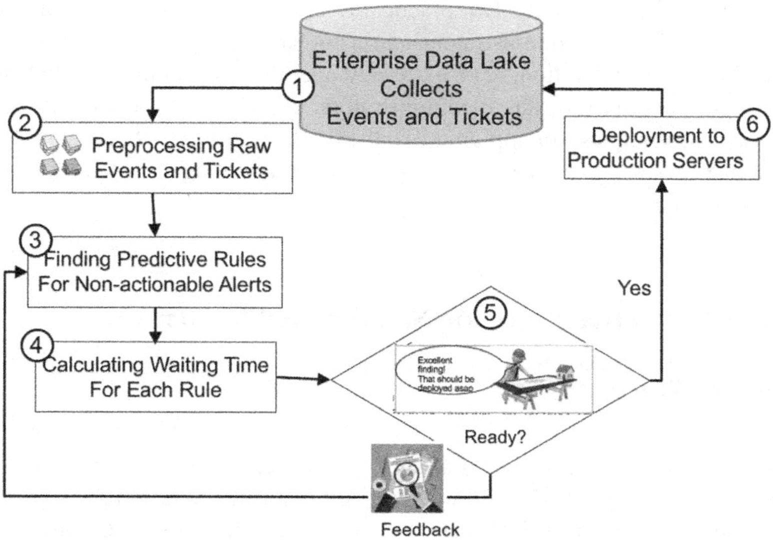


**Fig. 2** The overview of an off-line approach to eliminating non-actionable tickets

## *Solution Overview*

Our solution does not predict whether an alert is real or non- actionable. Instead, we decide whether to postpone the creation of the ticket or not, and how long is it to be postponed. Even if a real alert is incorrectly classified as non-actionable, its ticket will eventually be created before violating the service level agreement (SLA).

There are two key problems in this approach:

- How to identify whether an alert is non-actionable or real?
- If an alert is identified as non-actionable, what waiting time should be applied before ticket creation? (Fig. 2)

To solve the above two problems, we follow an approach that is described below. Recent events and monitoring tickets, collected in the data lake, are preprocessed for a search for predictive rules to build the non-actionable alert predictor, followed by calculation of the waiting time. After a feedback provided by the system administrators, the predictive rules and the waiting time are deployed to production servers. Later, the data lake collects new events and tickets to be used in subsequent learning cycles. This creates a continuously evolving system for eliminating false positive tickets. As the processing loop is designed for a once-a-month approach, all processes in the system are off-line .

Our work is based on off-line learning. The configurations of production systems are known to change as often as every 1 or 3 months. This is the reason for a monitoring life cycle process where the effectiveness of the monitoring configuration is re-assessed quarterly. Day-to-day operation is not suitable for our static network and system, because there are two practical issues: (1) One day's alerts and tickets are very few, so system administrators would not have enough confidence to change the monitoring configuration. (2) Day-to-day operation would increase the amount of unnecessary work for system administrators, because every learned rule would trigger a change request for applying it to the production server. In case of an unexpected event burst it is possible to run our solution again when the system administrators detect it.

## Finding Predictive Rules for Non-actionable Alerts

### *Predictive Rules*

The alert predictor roughly assigns a label to each alert, "non- actionable" or "real". It is built on a set of predictive rules that are automatically generated by a rule-based learning algorithm [3] based on historical events and alert tickets. Example 1 is an example of the predictive rule, where "*PROC CPU TIME*" is the CPU usage of a process. "*PROC NAME*" is the name of the process.

*Example 1* ***if*** *PROC CPU TIME > 50%* ***and*** *PROC NAME = 'htcscan',*

***then*** *this alert is non-actionable.*

A predictive rule consists of a rule condition and an alert label. A rule condition is a conjunction of *literals*, where each *literal* is composed of an event attribute, a relational operator and a constant value. In Example 1, "*PROC CPU TIME > 50%*" and "*PROC NAME = 'htcscan'*" are two *literals*, where "*PROC CPU TIME*" and "*PROC NAME*" are event attributes, ">" and "=" are relational operators, and "50%" and "*htcscan*" are constant values. If an alert event satisfies a rule condition, we call this alert covered by this rule. Since we only need predictive rules for non-actionable alerts, the alert label in our case is always "non-actionable".

### *Predictive Rule Generation*

The rule-based learning algorithm first creates all *literals* by scanning historical events. Then, it applies a breadth-first search for enumerating all *literals* in finding predictive rules, i.e., those rules having predictive power. This algorithm has two criteria to quantify the minimum predictive power: the minimum confidence $minconf$ and the minimum support $minsup$. In our case, $minconf$ is the minimum ratio of the numbers of non-actionable alerts and of all alerts covered by the rule, and $minsup$ is the minimum ratio of the number of alerts covered by the rule and the total number of alerts. For example, $minconf = 0.9$ and $minsup = 0.1$, then for each predictive rule found by the algorithm, at least 90% covered historical alerts are non-actionable, and at least 10% historical alerts are covered by this rule. Therefore, this rule has a certain predictive power for non-actionable alerts. The two criteria govern the performance of our method, defined as the total number of removed non-actionable alerts. To achieve the best performance, we loop through the values of *minconf* and *minsup* and compute the performance for each pair.

## Predictive Rule Selection

According to the Service Level Agreement (SLA), real tickets must be acknowledged and resolved within a certain time. Our method has to know the maximum allowed time for postponing a ticket. In addition, for each monitoring situation, our method also needs to know the maximum ratio of real tickets that can be postponed, which is mainly determined by the severity of the situation. Therefore, there are two user-oriented parameters:

- The maximum ratio of real alerts that can be delayed, *ratiodelay*, $0 \leq ratiodelay \leq 1$.
- The maximum allowed delay time for any real alert, *delaymax*, $aymax \geq 0$.

*ratiodelay* and *delaymax* are specified by the system administrators according to the severity of the monitoring situation and the SLA. Although the predictive rule learning algorithm can learn many rules from the training data, we only select those with strong predictive power. Laplace accuracy is a widely used measure for estimating the predictive power of a rule [4–6], which is defined as follows:

$$LaplaceAccuracy\left(c_i, \mathcal{D}\right) = \frac{N\left(c_i\right)+1}{N_{non}+2},$$

where $\mathcal{D}$ is the set of alert events, *ci* is a predictive rule, *N*(*ci*) is the number of events in $\mathcal{D}$ satisfying rule *ci*, and *Nnon* is the total number of non-actionable events in $\mathcal{D}$. Laplace accuracy estimates conditional probability [5, 6], so for example, if a rule *c*1 in $\mathcal{D}$ has *LaplaceAccu*(*c*1,$\mathcal{D}$) = 0.9, it implies that given an alert *e* which is covered by *c*1, the probability that *e* is non-actionable is 0.9.

Another issue in selecting predictive rules is rule redundancy. For example, let us consider the two predictive rules:

X. *PROC CPU TIME* > 50% ***and*** *PROC NAME* = 'thcscan'
Y. *PROC CPU TIME* > 60% ***and*** *PROC NAME* = 'thcscan'

Clearly, if an alert satisfies Rule Y, then it must satisfy Rule X as well. In other words, Rule Y is more specific than Rule X. If Rule Y has a lower accuracy than Rule X, then Rule Y is redundant given Rule X (but Rule X is not redundant given Rule Y). In our work, we perform redundant rule pruning to discard the more specific rules with lower accuracies.

### *Why Choose a Rule-based Predictor?*

First, each monitoring situation is equivalent to a quantitative association rule, so the predictor can be directly implemented in the existing event management system. Other classification algorithms are very difficult to implement as monitoring situations in real systems. The second reason is that a rule-based predictor facilitates feedback from a system administrator. In contrast, to a rule, like Example 1 above, a linear/non-linear equation or a neural network formed by several system attributes is very hard for a person to verify.

## Calculating Waiting Time for Each Rule

Waiting time is the duration by which tickets should be postponed if their corresponding alerts are classified as non- actionable. It is not unique for one monitoring situation. Since an alert can be covered by different predictive rules, we set up different waiting times for each of them.

In order to remove as many non-actionable alerts as possible, we set the waiting time of a selected rule as the longest duration of the transient alerts covered by it. For a selected predictive rule *p*, its waiting time is

$$wait_p = \max_{e \in \mathcal{F}_p} e.duration,$$

where

$$\mathcal{F}_p = \{e |, e \in \mathcal{F} |, isCovered(p,e) =' true'\},$$

and F is the set of transient events. Clearly, for any rule $p \in \mathscr{P}$, $waitp \leq delaymax$. Therefore, no ticket can be postponed for more than *delaymax*.

### *Differentiation*

A significant amount of work in data mining has been done to identify actionable patterns of events. Different types of patterns, such as (partially) periodic patterns, event bursts, and mutually dependent patterns were introduced to describe system management events. Efficient algorithms were developed to find and interpret such patterns. Our work is based on the part of an event processing workflow that takes into account the human processing of the tickets. This allowed us to identify non-actionable patterns and misses of the monitoring system configuration with significant precision. In the event processing workflow, false positive events are transformed into false positive tickets. Identification of false positive events makes it possible to significantly reduce the number of false positive tickets.

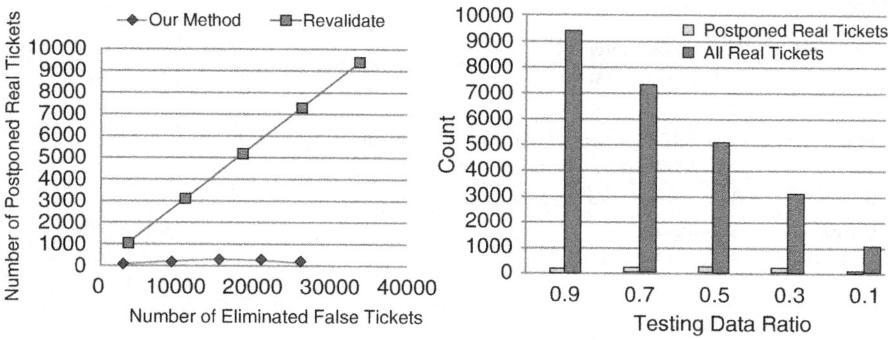


**Fig. 3** (**a**) Comparison with Revalidate . (**b**) Postponed real tickets

Based on the experience of the system administrators, we set $delay_{max} = 240$ min for all monitoring situations. Figure 3 presents the experimental results. Our method eliminates more than 75% of the false alerts and only postpones less than 3% of the real tickets (Fig. 3b).

Comparing with Revalidate [14]: Since most alert detection methods cannot guarantee complete absence of false positives, we compare our method with Revalidate, which revalidates the status of events and postpones all tickets. Revalidate has only one parameter, the postponement time, which is the maximum allowed delay time $delay_{max}$. Figure 3a compares the respective performance of our method and Revalidate, where each point corresponds to a different test data ratio. While Revalidate is clearly better in terms of elimination of false alerts, it postpones all real tickets, the postponement volume being 1000–10,000 times larger than our method. Reduced delay time is critical for QoS under SLA.

# Ticket Analysis and Resolution

## *Challenges and Proposed Solutions*

The Incident, Problem, and Change (IPC) system facilitates the tracking, analysis and mitigation of problems. Each ticket is stored as a database record that consists of several related attributes (see Table 1 for the major attributes) and of their values along with the system status at the time this ticket was generated. Some of the major attributes, such as the ticket summary (created by the aggregation of the system status and containing the problem description) and the ticket resolution (the textual description of the solution) are critical for diagnosing and resolving similar tickets. Service providers provide an account for every beneficiary that uses the services on a common IT infrastructure.

With increasing complexity and scalability of IT services, the necessity of a large-scale efficient workflow in IT service management is undeniable. The samples

**Table 1** Sample tickets

| **Severity** | **First-occurrence** | **Last-occurrence** |
|---|---|---|
| 0 | 2014-03-29 05:50:39 | 2014-03-31 05:36:01 |
| **Summary** | ANR2579E Schedule INC0630 in domain VLAN1400 for node LAC2APP2204XWP failed (return code 12) | |
| **Resolution** | Backups are working fine for the server. | |
| **Cause** | **Actionable** | **Last-update** |
| Maintenance | Actionable | 2014-04-29 23:19:25 |

**Table 2** Samples of ticket's summary and resolution

| ID | Summary | Resolution |
|---|---|---|
| 1 | Box getFolderContents BoxServerException | User doesnt have proper BOX account |
| 2 | Box getFolderContents BoxServerException | User should access box terms before access the efile site |
| 3 | Box getFolderContents BoxServerException | Resolved |
| 4 | High space used for logsapp | Resolved |
| 5 | High space used for disk C | 5.24 GB free space present |

of real-world tickets (see Table 2 for the contents of tickets that are not easily interpretable) illustrate the unique ticket features that are less intuitive and lead to challenges in IT service management, especially in automated ticket resolution analysis. Here we describe two key challenges in automating ticket resolution.

**Challenge1** How to quantify the quality of the ticket resolution?

Earlier studies generally assumed that the tickets with similar descriptions should have similar resolutions, and often treated all such ticket resolutions equally. However, the study [13] demonstrated that not all of the resolutions are equally worthy. For example, as shown in Table 2, the resolution text "resolved" is not useful at all. As a result, the quality of "resolved" is much lower than other resolutions. In order to develop an effective resolution recommendation model, such low-quality resolutions should be ranked lower than high-quality resolutions. In our proposed framework, we first carefully identify relevant features and then build a regression model to quantify ticket resolution quality.

**Challenge 2** How to make use of the historical tickets along with their resolution quality for effective automation of IT service management?

Although, it might be intuitive to search for historical tickets with the most similar ticket summary, and recommend their resolutions as potential solutions to the target ticket [13], such an approach might not be effective due to (1) the difficulty in representing the ticket summary and resolution, and (2) the avoidance of the resolution quality quantification. It is an essential task in IT service management to accurately represent the ticket summary and resolution. The classical techniques such as the n-gram, TF-IDF, and LDA are not effective in representing tickets as the ticket summary and resolution are generally not well formatted. In our proposed framework, we train a deep neural network ranking model using tickets along with their quality scores obtained from the resolution quality quantification. The ranking model directly outputs the matching scores of ticket summary and resolution pairs. Given an incoming incident, the historical resolutions having top matching scores with its ticket summary can then be recommended. In addition, the feature vectors derived from the ranking model provide effective representations for the tickets and can be used in other ticket analysis tasks, such as ticket classification and clustering.

## Ticket Resolution Quality Quantification

In this section, we describe the features used to quantify the quality of ticket resolutions and present several interesting findings from our experiments.

A ticket resolution is a textual attribute of a ticket. A high quality ticket resolution is supposed to be well written and informative enough to describe the detailed actions taken to fix the problem specified in the ticket summary. A low-quality ticket resolution is less or non-informative and is mostly logged by a careless system administrator or when the corresponding issue described in the ticket is negligible. Based on our long preliminary study [13], we've found that for a typical ticket, the ticket resolution quality is driven by the 33 features that can be broadly divided into following four groups:

- Character-level features: A low-quality ticket resolution might include a large number of unexpected characters, such as space, wrong or excessive capitalization, and special characters.
- Entity-level features: A high-quality ticket resolution is expected to provide information on IT-related entities, such as server name, le path, IP address, and so forth. Because the ticket resolutions are expected to guide system administrators to solve the problem specified in the ticket summary, the presence of the context- relevant entities makes the resolution text more useful.
- Semantic-level features: A high-quality ticket resolution typically includes Verb and Noun, which explicitly guides system administrators on the actions taken to diagnose the problem and to resolve the ticket.
- Attribute-level features: A high-quality ticket resolution usually is lengthy enough to carry sufficient information relevant to the problem described in the ticket summary.

The ticket resolution quality quantifier uses these four groups of features and operates on the historical tickets to output a set of triplets as ticket summary, ticket resolution and the quality score assigned by the quantifier.

## Feature Description

**Character-level features** To quantify the use of character usage, we considered each of the nine character classes (exclamationRatio, colonRatio, bracketRatio, @ Ratio, digitRatio, uppercaseRatio, lowercaseRatio, punctuationRatio, whitespaceRatio) as a feature and then computed their frequency to all the characters within the ticket resolution.

**Entity-level features** To quantify the usage of IT related entities, we considered each of the eight entity classes (numericalNumber, percentNumber, lepathNumber, dateNumber, timeNumber, ipNumber, servernameNumber, className) as a feature and computed their frequency to all the words within the ticket resolution. The occurrence of these entities was captured using regular expressions. For example, the lepathNumber refers to the total number of occurrences of Linux and Window le path in the ticket resolution. For the className, we considered the total number of occurrences of class names or functions in the programming languages, such as Java, Python, and so forth. Other entities that we explored had negligible contribution to the overall model performance in comparison with these enteties.

**Semantic-level features** To quantify the usage of those specific semantic words, we first preprocessed every ticket resolution into a Part-Of-Speech (PoS) [10] tag sequence and then calculated the ratio of each tag within the tag sequence. We defined features based on 12 meaningful tags in the NTLK implementation [2], such as VERBRatio, NOUNRatio, PRONRatio, ADJRatio, ADVPNRatio, ADPRatio, CONJRatio, DETRatio, NUMRatio, PRTRatio, PUNCTRatio, XRatio. Furthermore, we borrowed the concepts, such as, Problem, Activity and Action from work [11], but reduced them into two concepts merging Activity into Action. We used the regular expressions to calculate the occurrence of each concept feature problem Num, action Num.

**Attribute-level features** To quantify the high-quality resolution in a ticket, we included two attribute-level features resolution- Length, interSimilarity in our model. The first one was used for the ticket resolution length. The second one was used to record the Jaccard similarity between a ticket's summary and its resolution, and was used to define the relevance between them.

## Findings

We evaluated three of the most popular regression models (logistic regression, gradient boosting tree and random forest [1]) on the labeled real-world ticket dataset and found that the random forest performed best for the ticket resolution quantification and also for evaluation of the feature importance.

Based on our evaluation, we found that the best indicator of a good resolution was the length of the resolution resolutionLength, followed by the occurrence of the concept action, i.e., feature actionNum. It is also self-intuitive that the long resolution can be more informative. The features actionNum and problemNum correspond to the problems identified and the actions taken by the system administrators in the process of resolving the ticket.

Another interesting finding was that seven out of the top 15 features belonged to the group word level semantic features, and were specifically derived from the PoS tag sequence. The third top- ranked feature was PRTRatio related to the ratio of the words tagged as particle or function words. This implied that the resolutions containing the function words such as "for" and "due to" have a high quality. Moreover, high-quality resolutions were usually well written and complied with the natural language syntax, while the low-quality resolutions, on the other hand, were ill-formatted and caused great difficulty for the PoS tagger trained on natural languages. In summary, the semantic features have predominant advantages in characterizing and quantifying the ticket resolution quality over the other features.

## Deep Neural Ranking Model

In our preliminary work [13], we model the automating ticket resolution task as an information retrieval problem and tackle it from the perspective of finding a similar ticket summary in historical data, in which we treat each ticket resolution equally. However, given the triplets described earlier, we improve the automating ticket resolution task by considering the quality of resolutions.

We view the automating ticket resolution task as a text pair ranking task, which is one of the most popular tasks in the information retrieval (IR) domain.

The ticket with the same ticket summary can be resolved by multiple resolutions with different qualities. In automating ticket resolution, we expect the model to recommend all the possible resolutions, but with the order in which high quality resolution ranks first. Therefore, given the triplets described above the goal is to build a model that for ticket summary generates an optimal ranking score for each resolution, such that a relevant resolution with a high quality has a high ranking score.

We adopt the simple pointwise ranking model and focus more on modeling the representation for a ticket and its components using deep learning techniques.

We use the vector representation for ticket summary and for ticket resolution, derived from our sentence model for the automation of IT service management, also for ticket clustering and ticket classification.

## Differentiation

Overall performance results against known alternatives are shown in Table 3. We have some interesting observations from the results. The performance of the generative methods is quite moderate. The automatic resolution generators tend to produce

**Table 3** Overall performance comparison with systems described in this section

| System | p1 | MAP | nDCG5 | nDCG10 |
|---|---|---|---|---|
| SMT | 0.421 | 0.324 | 0.459 | 0.501 |
| LSTM-RNN | 0.563 | 0.367 | 0.572 | 0.628 |
| Random shuffle | 0.343 | 0.273 | 0.358 | 0.420 |
| CombinedLDAKNN | 0.482 | 0.347 | 0.484 | 0.536 |
| Our method | **0.742** | **0.506** | **0.628** | **0.791** |

universal, trivial and ambiguous resolutions which are likely to resolve a wide range of tickets, but not specific enough to conduct a meaningful remediation on faulted servers, i.e., low quality resolutions. This leads to the overwhelming performance of retrieved methods over generative methods.

When it comes to phrase based SMT, it is very tricky to segment large parts of ticket summaries into meaningful words or phrases since they are automatically generated by machines and can be extremely noisy. In general, generative approaches using deep learning (LSTM-RNN) outperform those without deep learning techniques and more advantage can be gained using input with character level order information.

## Auto-resolving Actionable Tickets

### *Challenges and Solution*

The goal of any automation is to handle isolated anomalies as well as complex syndromes manifested by business workload performance degradation. Simple events are already handled by many automation engines mostly through direct mapping of an event type to a specific automation script and in some cases, direct mapping substituted by simple rules. Handling complex issues is typically left to a human. Below we discuss a service that provides recommendations for resolutions to simple events as well as complex syndromes.

We model the automation recommendation procedure of IT automation services as a contextual bandit problem with dependent arms, where the arms are in the form of hierarchies. Intuitively, different automations in IT automation services, designed to automatically solve the corresponding ticket problems, can be organized into a hierarchy by domain experts according to the types of ticket problems. We introduce the hierarchical multi-armed bandit algorithms leveraging the hierarchies, which can match the coarse- to-fine feature space of arms. Empirical experiments on a real large-scale ticket dataset have demonstrated substantial improvements over the conventional bandit algorithms. In addition, a case study of dealing with the cold-start problem (reasoning about issues for which there is no sufficient information) is conducted to clearly show the merits of our proposed algorithms.

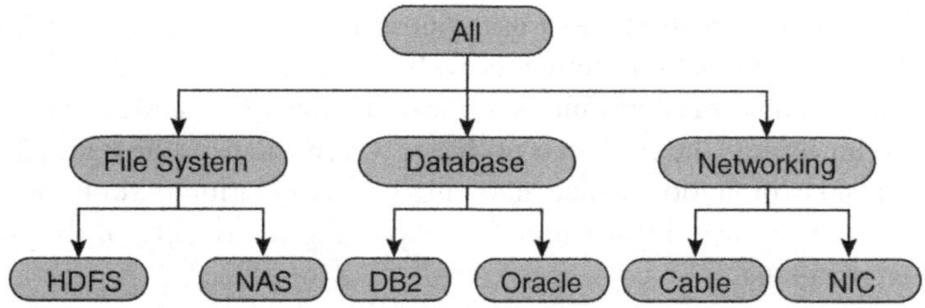


**Fig. 4** An example of taxonomy in IT tickets

**Challenge 1** How do we utilize the interactive feedback to adaptively optimize the recommending strategies of the enterprise automation engine to enable a quick problem determination by IT automation services?

The automation engine (see Fig. 1) automatically takes action based on the contextual information of the ticket and observes the execution feedback (e.g., success or failure) from the problem server. The current strategies of the automation engine do not take advantage of this interactive information for continuous improvement. Based on the aforementioned discussion, we present an online learning problem of recommending an appropriate automation and constantly adapting the up-to-date feedback given the context of the incoming ticket. This can be naturally modeled as a contextual multi-armed bandit problem, which has been widely applied into various interactive recommender systems [8, 12, 13].

**Challenge 2** How do we efficiently improve the performance of recommendations using the automation hierarchies of IT automation services?

Domain experts usually define the taxonomy (i.e., hierarchy) of the IT problems explicitly (see Fig. 4). Correspondingly, the scripted resolutions (i.e., automations) also contain the underlying hierarchical problems' structure.

For example, a ticket is generated due to a failure of the DB2 database. The root cause may be database deadlock, high usage or other issues. Intuitively, if the problem was initially categorized as a database problem, the automated ticket resolutions have a much higher probability to fix this problem, than if it hasn't been categorized as such, and all other categories (e.g., file system and networking) are now taken into consideration. We formulate this as a contextual bandit problem with dependent arms organized hierarchically, which can match the feature spaces from a coarse level first, and then be refined to the next lower level of taxonomy. The existing bandit algorithms can only explore the flat feature spaces by assuming the arms are independent.

**Challenge 3** How do we appropriately solve the well- known cold-start problem in IT automation services? Most recommender systems suffer from a cold-start problem. This problem is critical since every system could encounter a significant number of users/items that are completely new to the system with no historical records at all. The cold-start problem makes recommender systems ineffective unless additional information about users/items is collected [7, 9], which is a crucial problem for automation engine as well, since it cannot make any effective recommendation that translates into significant human efforts. Multi-armed bandit algorithms can address the cold-start problem, which balances the tradeoff between exploration and exploitation, hence, maximizing the opportunity for fixing the tickets, while gathering new information for improving the quality of the ticket and automation matching.

**Solution**

The key features of our input include:

- A new online learning approach, designed to (1) solve the cold-start problem, and (2) continuously recommend an appropriate automation for the in- coming ticket and adapt based on the feedback to improve the quality of match between the problem and automation in IT automation services.
- Utilization of the hierarchies, integrated into bandit algorithms to model the dependencies among arms.

We formalize the online IT automation recommendation process as a contextual multi-armed bandit problem where automations are constantly recommended and the underlying recommendation model is instantly updated based on the feedback collected over time. In general, a contextual multi-armed problem involves a series of decisions over a finite but possibly unknown time horizon T. In our formalization, each automation corresponds to an arm. Pulling an arm indicates its corresponding automation is being recommended, and the feedback (e.g., success or failure) received after pulling the corresponding arm is used to compute the reward.

In the contextual multi-armed bandit setting, at each time t between 1 and T, a policy π makes a decision for selecting an automation π(xt) ∈ A to perform an action according to the contextual vector xt of the current ticket. rk,t denotes the reward for recommending an automation $a^{(k)}$ at time t, whose value is drawn from an unknown distribution determined by the context xt presented to automation $a^{(k)}$. The total reward received by the policy π after T iterations is $R_\pi = \sum_{t=1}^{T} r_\pi(x_t)$..

The optimal policy π∗ is defined as the one with maximum accumulated expected reward after T iterations,

$$\pi^* = \arg\max_\pi E(R_\pi) = \arg\max_\pi \sum_{t=1}^{T} E(r_\pi(x_t)|t).$$

Our goal is to identify a good policy for maximizing the total reward. Herein we use reward instead of regret to express the objective function, since maximization of the cumulative reward is equivalent to minimization of regret during the T iterations [12].

Before selecting the optimal automation at time t, a policy π is updated to refine a model for reward prediction of each automation according to the historical observations. The reward prediction helps to ensure that the policy π includes decisions to increase the total reward. To address the aforementioned problem, contextual multi-armed bandit algorithms have been proposed to balance the tradeoff between exploration and exploitation for arm selection, including ε-greedy, Thompson sampling, LinUCB, etc.

Although different multi-armed bandit algorithms have been proposed and extensively adopted in diverse real applications, most of them do not take the dependencies between arms into account. In the IT environment, the automations (i.e., arms) are organized with its taxonomy, i.e., a hierarchical structure. The following section will introduce our approach to make use of the arm dependencies in the bandit settings for IT automation recommendation optimization. In IT automation services, the automations can be classified with a pre- defined taxonomy. It allows us to reformulate the problem as a bandit model with the arm dependencies described by a tree-structured hierarchy.

The goal is to recommend an automation for resolving a ticket. Since a leaf node in the taxonomy, which contains a set of nodes (i.e., arms) organized in a tree-structured hierarchy, represents an automation, the recommendation process cannot be completed until a leaf node is selected at each time. Therefore, the multi-armed bandit problem for IT automation recommendation is reduced to selecting a path in the taxonomy from root to a leaf node, where multiple arms along the path are sequentially selected with respect to the contextual vector at that time.

We use the HMAB (Hierarchical Multi-Armed Bandit) algorithms for exploiting the dependencies among arms organized hierarchically. As a ticket arrives, the evaluation procedure computes a score for each arm of different levels. In each level, the arm with the maximum score is selected to be pulled. After receiving a reward by pulling an arm, the new feedback is used to update the HMAB algorithms.

## *Differentiation*

To demonstrate the efficiency of our approach, we conduct a large scale experimental study over a real ticket dataset from IBM Global Services. First, we outline the general implementation of the baseline algorithms for comparison. Second, we describe the dataset and evaluation method. Finally, we discuss the comparative experimental results of the proposed and baseline algorithms, and present a case study to demonstrate the effectiveness of HMAB algorithms.

In order to better illustrate the merits of the proposed algorithms, we present a case study on the recommendation for an escalated ticket in IT automation services.

As mentioned above, the recommendation for an escalated ticket can be regarded as a cold-start problem due to the lack of corresponding automations. In other words, there are no historical records for resolving this ticket. Note that both our proposed HMABs and conventional MABs are able to deal with the cold-start problem by exploration. To compare their performance, we calculate the distribution of the recommended automations over different categories (e.g., database, unix, and application). Figure 6 presents an escalated ticket, which records a database problem. Such a problem has been repeatedly reported over time in the dataset.

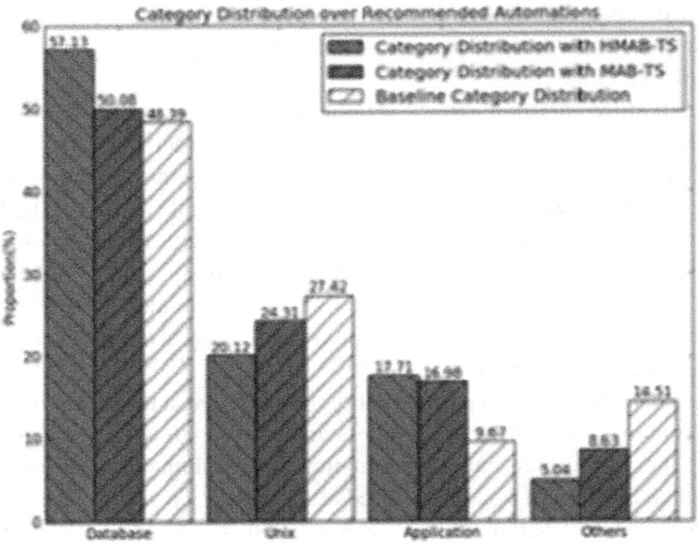


**Fig. 5** The comparison of categories for recommended automations

Since this ticket reports a database problem, intuitively the automations in the database category should have a high chance of being recommended. The category distributions of our proposed HMABs and conventional MABs are provided in Fig. 5, as well as the base- line category distribution, which is the prior category distribution obtained from all the automations of the hierarchy. From Fig. 5, we observe that (1) compared with TS, HMAB-TS explores more automations from the database category; and (2) in HMAB-TS the database category has the highest percentage among all the automation categories. This shows that our proposed HMABs can achieve better performance by making use of the predefined hierarchy.

To further illustrate the effectiveness of HMABs, we provide the detailed results of recommended automations for the escalated tickets. As shown in Fig. 6, automations from the database category (e.g., database instance down automation, db2 database in- active automation) are frequently recommended according to the context of the ticket, which clearly indicate the issue is due to the inactive database. By checking the recommended results, domain experts figure out the 'database instance down' automation, one of the top recommended automations, can successfully fix such a cold-start ticket problem, which clearly demonstrates the effectiveness of our proposed algorithms.

## Dataset Description

Experimental tickets are collected by the IBM Monitoring system. This dataset covers from July 2016 to March 2017 with the size of |D| = 116,429. Statistically, it contains 62 automations (e.g., NFS Automation, Process CPU Spike Automation,

| ALERT_KEY | all_dbinact_grs_std | AUTOMATION NAME | ESCALATION_1 |
|---|---|---|---|
| TICKET SUMMARY | Database allCCTd status is inactive | TICKET RESOLUTION | The database is down. It has been restarted, hence closing the ticket |

| Recommended Category | (%) | RECOMMENDED AUTOMATION |
|---|---|---|
| DATABASE | 57.13 | (1) database instance down; (2) MSSQL database inactive (3) Oracle database offline |
| UNIX | 20.12 | (1) space check diskgroup dbautomation; (2) hostdown automation; (3) certification expiration automation |
| APPLICATION | 17.71 | (1) ntp restart (2) mq manager down |
| OTHER | 5.04 | (1) system load automation (2) others |

**Fig. 6** The exploration by HMAB-TS of a cold-start ticket case

and Database Inactive Automation) recommended by the automation engine to fix the corresponding problems. The execution feedback includes success, failure and escalation, indicating whether the problem has been resolved or needs to be escalated to human engineers. This collected feedback can be utilized to improve the accuracy of recommended results. Thereby, the problem of automation recommendation can be regarded as an instance of the contextual bandit problem. As we mentioned above, an arm is an automation, a pull is to recommend an automation for an incoming ticket, the context is the information vector of the ticket's description, and the reward is the feedback on the result of the execution of recommended automation on the problem server. An automation hierarchy H shown in Fig. 7 with three layers constructed by domain experts is introduced to present the dependencies among automations. Moreover, each record is stamped with the open time of the ticket.

Recommendations provided at run time are available through framework insights for further analysis and standardization. Fig. 8 shows a customer specific dashboard with Action plan that includes automated resolution recommendations.

## Conclusion and Future Work

By the time this book will be published, we will be able to fully automate event automation flow to handle isolated anomalies as well as complex syndromes manifested by business workload performance degradation. Currently we are deploying an automated system that takes advantage of AI through feedback loop analysis of historical data, and continuously improved recommendation for automated resolution of complex syndromes. It first detects a syndrome by identifying a group of symptoms that potentially have a common root cause. It then enriches the syndrome information with probable root causes and their diagnostics. Subsequently the diagnostics are run on the systems which exhibited anomalous behavior. The data collected is used for the root cause disambiguation. Finally, the derived root cause is submitted to a Resolution Planning Engine (RPE). It returns an optimized plan of

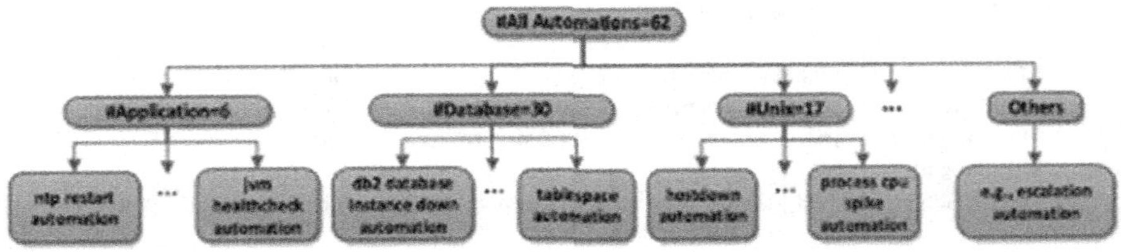


**Fig. 7** An automation hierarchy defined by domain experts

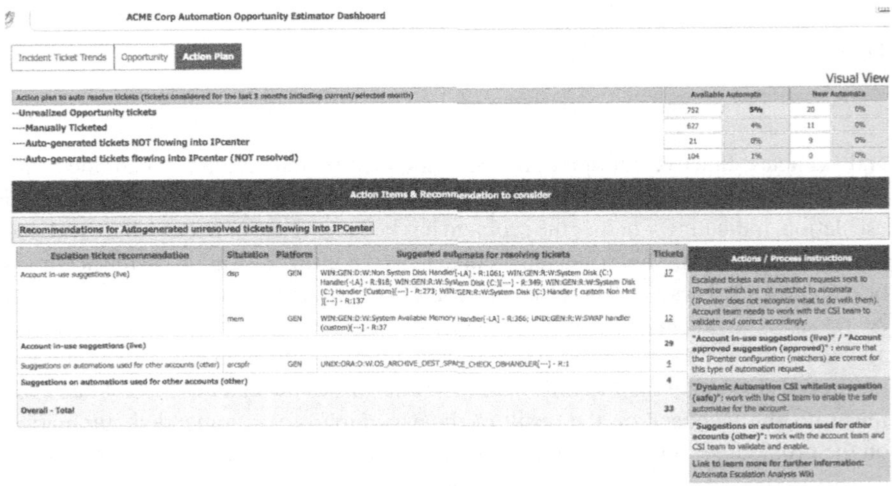


**Fig. 8** Opportunity estimator dashboard with resolution recommendations and action/instructions

actions for the remediation of the identified root cause. RPE is an AI (artificial intelligence) planner that uses cost-optimal planning with applications in plan recognition, diagnosis and explanation generation. Coordinated execution of the plan performed by appropriate automation engines on each segment of the hybrid environment. All details captured during resolution and healing of a complex symptom are stored in IBM's Data Lake and used by Cognitive Delivery Insights for further analysis and continual improvement across all of IBM's customers.

**Acknowledgements** Automating resolution of complex events is exciting but unknown territory for Service provides. We are grateful to the technical teams and executive leadership of IBM technical services for their trust and on-going support to our road to AI driven automation.

Also this work was done in collaboration with Florida International University and St. Johns University, and we thank our collaborators: prof. Dr. Tao Li (deceased), prof. Dr. G. Ya. Grabarnik, Dr. Liang Tang, Dr. C. Zeng, Dr. Wubai Zhou, and Qing Wang.

## References


1. Alpaydin E (2014) Introduction to machine learning. MIT Press, Cambridge
2. Bird S (2006) NLTK: the natural language toolkit. In: Proceedings of the COLING/ACL on Interactive presentation sessions. Association for Computational Linguistics, pp 69–72
3. Srikant R, Agrawal R (1996) Mining quantitative association rules in large relational tables. In: Proceedings of ACM SIGMOD, pp 1–12
4. Yin X, Han J (2003) CPAR: classification based on predictive association rules. In: Proceedings of SDM
5. Pazzani MJ, Merz CJ, Murphy PM, Ali K, Hume T, Brunk C (July 1994) Reducing misclassification costs. In: Proceedings of ICML, New Brunswick, NJ, pp 217–225
6. Li J (2006) Robust rule-based prediction. IEEE Trans Knowl Data Eng (TKDE) 18(8):1043–1054
7. Chang S, Zhou J, Chubak P, Hu J, Huang TS (2015) A space alignment method for cold-start tv show recommendations. In: Proceedings of the 24th International Conference on Artificial Intelligence, pp 3373–3379
8. Li L, Chu W, Langford J, Schapire RE (2010) A contextual-bandit approach to personalized news article recommendation. In: WWW. ACM, pp 661–670
9. Schein AI, Popescul A, Ungar LH, Pennock DM (2002) Methods and metrics for cold-start recommendations. In: SIGIR. ACM, pp 253–260
10. Petrov S, Das D, McDonald R (2011) A universal part-of-speech tagset. arXiv preprint arXiv:1104.2086.
11. Potharaju R, Jain N, Nita-Rotaru C (2013) Juggling the Jigsaw: towards automated problem inference from network trouble tickets. In: NSDI, pp 127–141
12. Zeng C, Wang Q, Mokhtari S, Li T (2016) Online context-aware recommendation with time varying multi- armed bandit. In: SIGKDD, pp 2025–2034
13. Zhou W, Tang L, Zeng C, Li T, Shwartz L, Ya Grabarnik G (2016) Resolution recommendation for event tickets in service management. IEEE Trans Netw Service Manag 13(4):954–967
14. Castillo LA, Mahaffey PD, Bascle JP (2008) Apparatus and method for monitoring objects in a network and automatically validating events relating to the objects. U.S. Patent, US 7,469,287 B1.

# Gaining Insight from Operational Data for Service Optimization

## Background

Service optimization is key in the drive to further automate and increase the effi-ciency of the services provided to clients. A given client may be ahead, in one or more areas, versus where other clients are. Learning from these best-of-breed cli-ents benefits the other clients in optimizing their services. Each of the clients normally generates a large number of data points for all the elements comprising the services they consume. Important data points are generally contained within incident tickets and change tickets. These tickets contain not only information about the nature of the issue, but also contain resolution information.

Comparing clients' service optimization positions and need for further automation, allows for identifying which additional automation opportunities need to be addressed first to achieve the highest yield. Comparison capabilities for incident tickets and resolution information across clients is required to achieve this goal. However, the information contained within these incident tickets is generally not structured nor standardized. This poses a challenge as normalization is required for classification and comparison reasons.

It should also be considered that, for the issues described in these incident tickets, a portion may be prevented as these are a direct result from changes to system configuration. This poses another challenge to identify the relationships between change tickets and the incident tickets caused by them.

The following chapter describe how each of these challenges is addressed.

 
K. Kloeckner et al., *Transforming the IT Services Lifecycle with AI Technologies*, SpringerBriefs in Computer Science,
https://doi.org/10.1007/978-3-319-94048-9_3

## Best of Breed and Opportunity Identification

### *Challenges*

Typically, a ticket is a record which has two parts: ticketed event information and information about resolution of this event. "Ticketed event" consists of several related attributes with values detailing the system state at the time the event was generated. For example, a CPU-related event usually contains the CPU utilization and paging utilization information. "Ticket resolution" contains a textual description of an approach taken by the system administrator toward resolution of the problem described in the event.

Best of Breed analysis across multiple accounts (for a service provider, or across industries) and Opportunity Identification for improved service automation is based on clustering and classification of tickets as they relate to automation (Fig. 1).

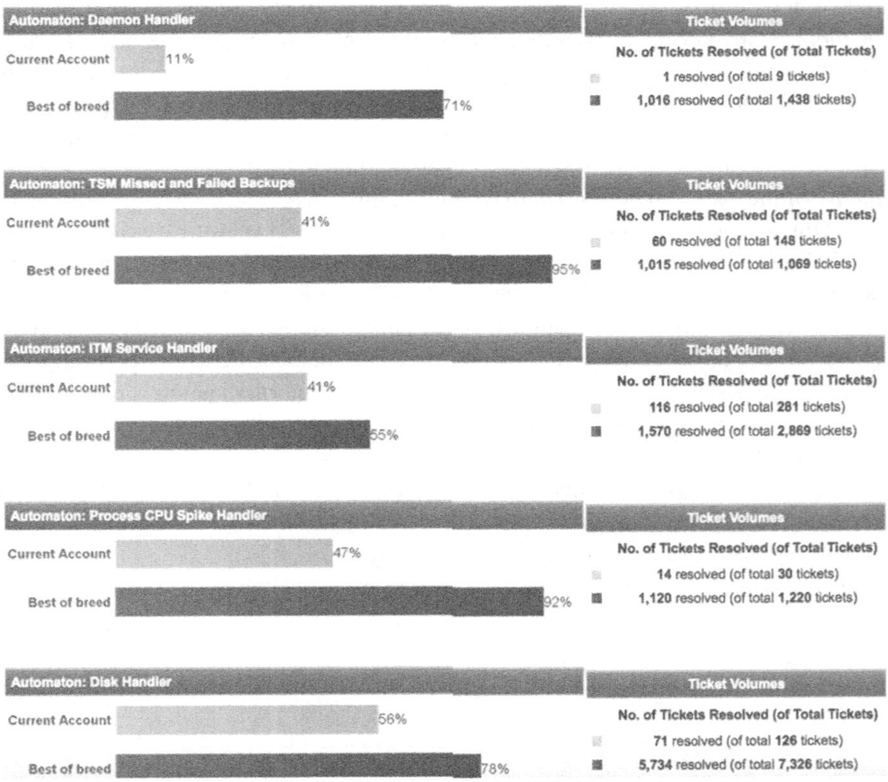


**Fig. 1** Best-of-breed Analysis compares the selected accounts' automation performance for selected problem areas with best of breed accounts' performance. This allows for identifying the relative position of the client with respect to service optimization

**Unique information in a ticket** Many researchers study and experiment on historical tickets in order to facilitate IT service optimization. In reality, however, large volumes of historical tickets are generated from large enterprise IT environments, and most of them are often manually examined and labeled, especially in the classic ticket clustering tasks. Ticket clustering provides important statistic information and also assists in the labeling process for supervised learning tasks in service managements. Today, IT service management heavily utilizes regular expressions on word features while manually inspecting ticket clusters. This activity is both labor intensive and error prone. On the other hand, some evidence suggests that ticket data is extremely noisy due to heterogeneity of server environments and limited useful root cause or resolution information. Typically, only two key textual attributes are considered to be important for featuring a ticket instance, i.e., attribute "SUMMARY/DESCRIPTION" in ticket event and "RESOLUTION" in ticket resolution. Noisy tickets could affect the quality of supervised tasks and in consequence harm the IT service automation. There is obviously a need for an unsupervised rule generation and noisy data removal process that can be fully automated and would benefit the downstream supervised tasks and would improve operational efficiency.

**Generic resolution of the ticket** In the Service Management chapter we described how we eliminate false positive alerts in a service management system. False positive alerts generate tickets which we call non-actionable tickets. These tickets usually do not have explicit or meaningful resolutions as they were created for a transient issue. The other common situation in which a useless resolution could be assigned to a ticket is when their root causes are difficult or cost-expensive to identify. In this scenario, system administrators would opt for resolving an issue without complete investigation of its causes. Commonly they will restart the server and assign resolution such as "restarted the server". Based on our experiments, on average at least 20% of monitoring tickets are non-actionable tickets. It is essential to remove tickets with these noisy resolutions from the dataset prior to clustering or classification exercise, and in general for any resolution recommendation task. We introduce the following definition of generic resolution:

**Definition 1** Generic Resolution is a non-informative resolution in a ticket that barely reveals information about the root cause, or a resolution that solves the problem by a general method which disregards the faulty state of the system or the workload and refreshes it to an initial state.

From the definition, it is safe to conclude that generic resolutions correlate little with their corresponding ticket summary since they are not designed to solve specific issues. Therefore, it is expected that tickets solved by a such resolution could be semantically dissimilar to each other.

**Noisy and limited unstructured data in tickets** Two tickets shown in Fig. 2 share some typical features such as "file", "capacity" and "delete" that show they both are about a "capacity full" problem, and they are highly correlated across all "capacity full" tickets. However, their distance measurement accuracy is affected by other noisy features. This problem is more severe when the text used for clustering is short.

## *Solution*

### Ticket Vectorization

Rather than using 'bag of words' directly on ticket data, certain preprocessing steps have been applied, such as removal of stop words and special characters, in order to vectorize tickets. Furthermore, we utilize regular expression matching to achieve word normalization on entities in the tickets. For the purpose of measuring similarity between tickets, entities such as file path, date and time are either removed or replaced by common strings. For instance, two tickets t1 and t2 relating to a "capacity full" issue both have a file system path with low capacity within the ticket content: Ticket t1: File system /ora/POSOA1p/backup01 is low and Ticket t2: File system /appldata/aexp/history2 is low. The specific file system path might jeopardize the clustering task. By replacing the path with a common string "filepathInst", both of these two tickets end up containing the same 'normalized' text. In our framework, the normalization on entities such as file, url, server(node) name, dates etc. is applied prior to clustering/classification.

After entity normalization, we use the bag of words methods for both ticket summary and ticket resolutions.

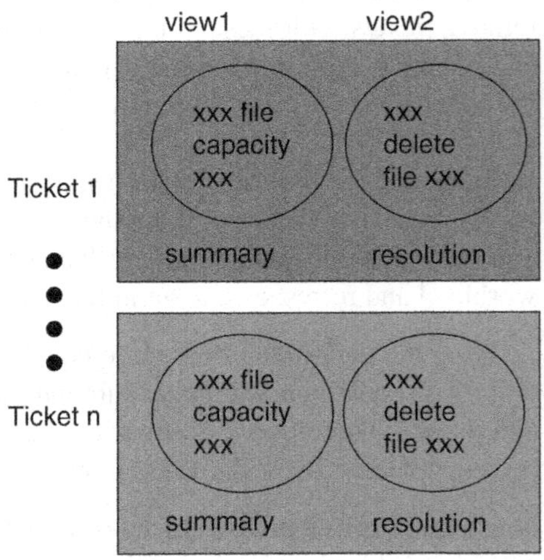


**Fig. 2** Keywords "file" and "capacity" in ticket summaries are highly correlated with keywords "delete" and "file", and they are the most informative words that can be used to correctly categorize the tickets if they are selected to represent the tickets and the noisy words presented as "xxx" are ignored

### Removing Tickets with Generic Resolutions

It is safe to assume that generic resolutions correlate little with their corresponding ticket summary since they are not designed to solve specific issues. Therefore, it is expected that tickets solved by such a resolution could be semantically dissimilar to each other. Based on this intuition, we implemented an effective two-step approach to remove tickets with generic resolutions.

1. Cluster tickets into groups according to their resolutions.
2. Further cluster tickets for each cluster on their summaries and obtain a consistency score of its summary clusters. Identify those resolutions with consistency score less than the threshold for generic resolutions.

Table 1 shows the top five low quality resolution clusters ranked by silhouette scores for their corresponding ticket summary clusters. As it was validated by domain experts, all these resolutions provide no clue to problem resolution, and they are considered to be generic resolutions. The tickets with these resolutions account for approximately 23% of all experimental tickets.

**Noisy tickets**

Since our tickets are represented by two views (i.e., "ticket event" and "ticket resolution"), we adapt a multi-view feature selection algorithm Sparse CCA (Classic Canonical Analysis) for further improving clustering. Proposed CCA can be viewed as addressing the problem of finding basis vectors for two sets of variables such that the correlation between the projections of the variables onto these basis vectors is mutually maximized.

In our work, we also use the sparse setup for Canonical Correlation Analysis to achieve the goal of feature selection from our noisy ticket dataset. Researchers proposed many efficient methods [1] to solve the sparse CCA problem. Here, we adopted the approach proposed by Julien et al. [1].

**Case Study**

We evaluated the effectiveness of our method through evaluating selected features with subject matter experts (SMEs). We listed the selected words from both ticket summaries and ticket resolutions as they appear in each pair. An example is captured in Table 2. The words highlighted in bold are key word features indicating the

**Table 1** The top five low quality resolution clusters ranked by silhouette scores

| Silhoueete score | Cluster size | Representative resolution |
|---|---|---|
| −0.0637 | 81 | Issue has been resolved. |
| −0.027 | 308 | Service started. |
| 0.01 | 227 | Issue has been resolved hence closing the ticket. |
| 0.0208 | 319 | Now sufficient space available. Hence closing the ticket |
| 0.088 | 99 | False alert. |

corresponding tickets' category as "Unix Disk Full". Moreover, highlighting these key words made system administrators very efficient in conducting ticket labeling.

**Clustering**
We also use Sparse CCA as dimensionality reduction techniques. For k pairs identified in the ticket, the ticket summary can be reduced to a k dimension vector (< a1, xi >, ..., < ak, xi >). Similarly, we apply this technique to the ticket resolution.

## *Differentiation*

To address these issues, we built a framework that handles noisy tickets and automatically selects word features for generating regular expressions, facilitating ticket clustering tasks with a minimal number of false positives. We first identify and remove the tickets with meaningless resolutions which build false correlation between tickets triggered by different events. Moreover, we adopt sparse Classic Canonical Analysis(CCA) to further conduct a feature selection task in order to facilitate expression generation. In summary, we contribute the following innovation:

- We established an effective and straightforward clustering-based approach to remove tickets with meaningless resolutions, which affect the automation of a ticket labeling process.
- We applied sparse Classic Canonical Analysis to simultaneously select key word features indicating the type of a ticket from ticket summary and resolutions, and adopted those words as candidates for regular expressions for an efficient ticket labeling.

Figure 3 shows results of clustering and classification for automation opportunity analysis for manual and monitoring tickets. The classification indicates which automation is already available (A) or which automation should be developed (N) as well as the volume that can be addressed. The prioritized list guides the account which opportunity is to be addressed first to make the biggest improvements in service optimization.

**Table 2** Sample keywords selected from the first (a, b) pair

| Summary | Resolution |
|---|---|
| cskpcloudxp oppr prd **low** czx-pap nzxppm | posbp orabkupnzapdb reduce ad Iv-tivoli iussue |
| wzxqap wcdc orabkup close **expire** szxpap | **drive zip hot backup high compress level** |
| izxdwb inode szxdap dcld drxpvm **clear** pzxp | **data** tivo-lifilesystem util app oracle increase |
| izxp opt szxnvm nzxp **tmp** szxp czxp wzxdap | housekeep clear alert free partition rman sda |
| critic **warn file** nzx-pap **usage** pzxnvm | control make **tmpfilesystem tmp file clean fs** |
| nzxpvm **percent linux use space high var** | **space expans nothing disk**. |

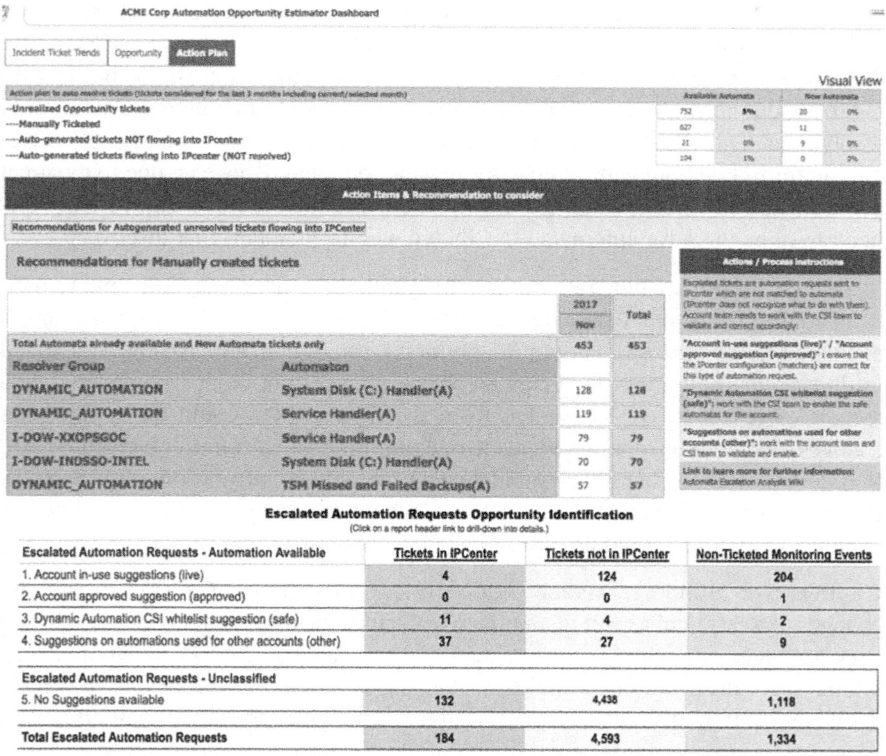


**Fig. 3** Automation opportunity dashboard

# Cognitive Analytics for Change

## *Challenges*

One of the biggest problems IT service providers face today is that significant number of incidents that result in client outages are reportedly caused by changes to the system configuration [2]. Despite the magnitude of this problem, the relationship between change and incident has historically been hard to establish [3]. There is a fair amount of research on analyzing incidents as well as changes. For example, incident analytics has been used to recommend resolutions for problems identified by monitoring [4], to classify server behavior to predict the impact of modernization actions [5], and to efficiently dispatch incident tickets in an IT service environment [6]. Similarly, change analytics has, for example, been used for change risk management [7] and to prevent changes from causing incidents by detecting conflicts among IT Change operations and safety constraints [8]. However, none of these approaches are addressing the problem of linking changes to incidents.

**Challenge 1** Establishing causality between changes and incidents. There is very little previous work on linking incidents to changes for incident prevention, partly because it is very difficult to systematically collect data on changes that lead to incidents due to the tremendous time pressure to quickly implement changes and resolve incidents. Root Cause Analysis (RCA) is another source of valuable information for linking incidents to changes that caused them. However, due to the great deal of detail in RCAs, which are mostly in unstructured text format, it is very difficult to mine them for automated CH IN (change-to-incident) link discovery.

In order to further illustrate our point regarding the importance of linking incidents to the changes that caused them, we show, in Fig. 4, all incidents and changes displayed for several accounts for a one-month timeframe. Changes are illustrated in dark color (blue), and incidents are illustrated in light color (yellow) rounded rectangles respectively. As evident from the figure, there could be hundreds of changes, and zero or more incidents happening for each account in a given month. In order to leverage change and incident data for incident prevention, it is necessary to at least semi-automatically link the incidents to the changes that caused them, as manual exploration would be fairly time consuming and often fruitless.

**Challenge 2** Building predictive models for preventing incidents caused by changes. An essential aspect of an effective Change Management process is Change Risk Management, which aims to assess and mitigate change risk to avoid change failures and, thus, minimize incidents causing disruption to the clients' business. While prevention of failed changes through risk management is very important and necessary, given the fairly small change failure rates (in our experience <1%), it does not seem to be the only answer to reducing client outages caused by changes.

**Challenge 3** Change Risk Prediction. Whenever a change to the IT infrastructure is required, a Change Analyst needs to assess the potential impact of the proposed change. Information available for assessment consists of, but is not limited to, the

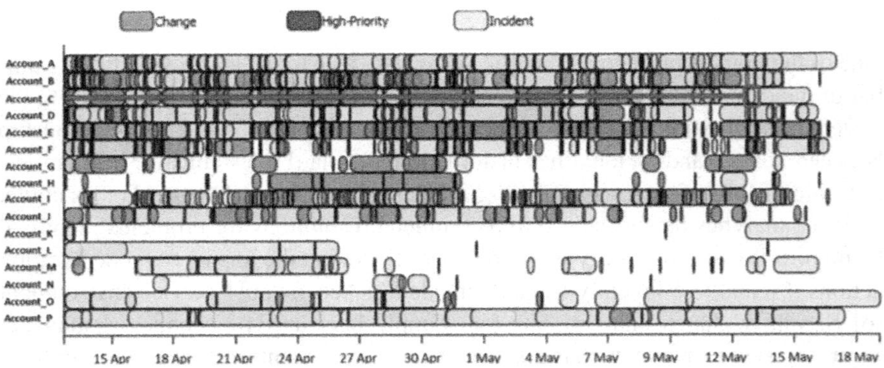


**Fig. 4** Change and incident dashboard for select accounts. Red circle highlights one incident (in yellow), and the arrow indicates the span of changes (in blue) that are potential candidates for having caused the incident

change description, details about the affected configuration items (such as a list of servers and their configuration), the team that will perform the change, and answers gathered to risk survey questions about the probability of change failure (e.g. how often was this change performed before) and the potential impact of change (e.g. how many business-critical processes and applications may be affected). Our framework leverages all this information from the change record being created as input to its Change Risk Prediction module.

## *Solution*

### Change Data

Change data describes change attributes such as summary, detailed description, start and end time, type, priority, owner group, implementation steps, verification plan, backout plan, approvers, and outcome (success, fail, backout) to name a few. Although the outcome attribute seems fairly useful, there is a major problem with using it to determine whether a change led to an incident or not. The change request outcome is determined at the time of change closing, which means that it reflects the correct information for failed or backed out changes, but not necessarily for successful changes. In other words, we cannot solely rely on the outcome attribute for linking changes to incidents as there are seemingly successful changes, which complete as designed, but lead to an incident later on (e.g., a patch successfully applied to a software could later cause the software to misbehave and cause an incident). Finally, backout changes, although backed out by design, may leave some residual risk, which may lead to an incident. The outcome attribute fails to capture such cases, and therefore does not prove to be a good indicator of whether the change led to an incident or not.

Another limitation with the change data is that failed changes are typically very small in number. Failed changes causing incidents are, thus, even smaller, which makes them not ideal for further studying incident causality. For that reason, in our study, we mainly focus on changes that are marked successful, but may have led to incidents.

### Configuration Data

In IT service delivery, configuration data is commonly used to maintain a current picture of the IT infrastructure used to deliver services. A configuration item (CI) is a unit that describes an item involved in the service delivery process. Examples of CIs include servers, databases, middleware, software, and business applications. A configuration management system (CMDB) inventories and manages the life-cycle of all CIs in an IT infrastructure environment. Typically, changes and incidents are related to one or more configuration items.

## Data Discovery and Clean-Up

Before we begin to analyze the data, we go through a data discovery and clean-up process. In this phase, the goal is to gather as much relevant information as possible about incidents and changes from the available data to build the data set for our investigation of change and incident causality.

### Structured Fields

Many structured fields exist for changes and incidents, but for our purpose, we selectively focus on the following after eliminating fields that are either mostly blank or have the same data (e.g., all FALSE):

Change: Start Time, Priority, Type, Owner Group
Incident: Summary, Detailed Description, Resolution Start Time, Severity, Type, Resolver Group

### Unstructured Fields

Similarly, for unstructured fields, we focus on the following after eliminating sparsely populated fields. We collectively call the change and incident related unstructured data "change text" and "incident text" respectively:

ChangeText: Summary,DetailedDescription
Incident Text: Summary, Detailed Description, Resolution

Explicit Mention: A small minority of incident texts mention the change that led to the incident. We need to extract this valuable information for later use as ground truth to test the accuracy of our CH IN linking methodology. For this, we use regular expression patterns and parse the incident text to extract the mentioned changes in incidents.

Discovering (Entity, Action) Pairs: Given the length and the complexity of unstructured fields, we extract (entity, action) pairs from change descriptions to help with linking changes to incidents. The idea is that the (entity, action) pairs would act as a classification as well as a summary of the change for a relatively easier comparison to the unstructured incident description and resolution. Example:

Change (entity, action) (server CMT01NAW1, reboot)

Incident resolution "After change rebooted the server CMT01NAW1 with success, we found the following error event on DC's that was impacted…".

To extract (entity, action) pairs, we use the Stanford NLP Dependency Parser [9] and look for noun phrases within the change summary. Once noun phrases are identified, we then look for the verbs associated with the noun phrase and take the top ranked pair among any multiple pairs. Figure 2 shows the sample actions extracted from ~650 change tickets that led to incidents for a given account. Entities are not displayed in order not to clutter the figure.

Common Words: Although (entity, action) pairs can be very definitive in connecting changes to incidents when the change (entity, action) is present in the incident text, the free-form nature of change and incident text makes it very unlikely for the exact change entity to be present in the incident text. In the example, Change (entity, action) (application server memory parameters, adjust), if we rely on the (entity, action) pair alone to link an incident to a change, unless the entity "application server memory parameters" appears in the incident text in its entirety, there will not be a match. On the other hand, however, "application server", or "memory parameters" or some other meaningful substring of the entity will often be sufficient to link the change to the incident. For that reason, we also determine the number of common words between change text and incident text as another indicator of the connection between changes and incidents.

Discovering CIs: In rare cases, a structured field may describe the CIs affected by the incident or change respectively. However, quite often, the system admin creating the incident or change ticket will not call out the CI in a separate field, but simply mention it as part of the change or incident text. Thus, we additionally employ text matching to identify all the CIs associated with a change or incident. For this purpose, we assume that an inventory of all CIs is available to us in some form (e.g., a CMDB or even just spreadsheets).

**Putting it together for establishing CH to IN linkage** Based on manual examination of available change and incident data, we consider the following dimensions as potential indicators of causality between changes and incidents:

- Time: time elapsed between change and incident
- SameCI: whether the change and incident happened on the same CI, e.g., (server XYZ)
- SameType: whether the change and incident have the same Type, e.g., (SAP instance)
- SameGroup: whether the change owner group is the same as the incident resolver group
- SameImpact: whether the change risk is the same as the incident risk
- SameEntityAction: whether the change (entity, action) pair exists in incident text
- NumberCommonWords: the number of common words between change and incident text

Once the data set is established using the above methods, it is possible to test the candidate dimensions for their contribution to CH to IN linkage.

When studying the change and incident data, the most intuitive dimension to consider is time. It is reasonable to assume that the change that led to the incident was implemented shortly before the incident. However, analysis of our (CH IN) pairs show that, for our data set, only 3% of the time, the incident took place within an hour of when the change was implemented; and only 11% of the time, the offending change was implemented within the same day of the incident.

Next, we tested the significance of using the other dimensions we had defined (see Putting it Together) based on our domain expertise and intuition. Including all dimensions provided a major improvement over using time alone.

**Predicting Failed Changes** Our goal is to investigate the role of change in incident reduction through a detailed study of the change-incident relationship. Traditionally, the focus of change risk management is on failed changes with the expectation that reducing failures would reduce incidents. However, our analysis, in Sections II B and C, revealed that, for the most part, it is the seemingly successful changes that lead to incidents. With this insight, before diving into predictive modeling, we first wanted to test the effectiveness of the traditional methodology, i.e. whether failed change predictors also identify incident inducing changes.

*Model 1* We selected an equal number of Failed and Successful changes for the training and testing datasets, and also additionally ensured that each category {Successful vs. Failed} had an equal number of {Incident vs. No_Incident} cases to remove any bias. We then trained and tested a predictive model using several different machine learning algorithms, however, for our data set, the Classification and Regression (C&R) Tree method [8] gave us the best recall rates. The C&R Tree models used were constructed using IBM SPSS with predictors such as owner group, change category, change priority, change risk, as well as derived change properties (such as change configuration item and change action) to predict if the input change is likely to fail. SPSS automatically performs feature selection to only use the significant predictive data fields. Testing is also performed through SPSS by using k-fold cross validation. The resulting model was statistically significant ($p < .005$), which indicates that the predictors reliably distinguished between changes that failed and changes that did not fail. We then inspected the test changes and compared their predicted outcomes to their observed outcomes to calculate:

(a) *recall rate* (i.e., how many of the failed test changes were correctly captured as 'failed' by the predictive model)
(b) *accuracy* (i.e., how many of the total set of test changes had correct prediction of their actual outcome – 'successful' or 'failed').

*Model 2* Our second predictive model is focused directly on incidents, namely whether a given change is likely to cause an incident irrespective of if fails or succeeds. For this model, we updated our testing and training datasets to differentiate incident causing changes from non-incident causing ones. We then trained and tested a C&R Tree model with the same predictors as before (see Table 3 for results).

*Model 3* Our third predictive model focuses on proactively identifying problematic changes (which comprise all failed changes as well as successful changes that led to an incident). For this model, we updated our test and training data sets to differentiate between problematic and non-problematic changes. We then trained and tested the C&R Tree model with the same predictors.

Figure 5 summarizes datasets used for three models.

## Risk Prediction Algorithm

A. Predictive Algorithm Design Considerations.

During the predictive algorithm design process, we tried various machine learning models, however, we decided to go with a statistical algorithm instead due to the following restrictions:

(a) Unbalanced Data: The number of problematic changes (even with the addition of changes that cause incidents) remain fairly low compared to the successful change volume (exact numbers cannot be disclosed due to confidentiality). The heavily unbalanced nature of the data makes it unideal for machine learning models. Although there is a lot of research on building predictive models on unbalanced data [9, 10], proposed techniques mainly work on static models built out of training data sets and updated manually. Because COACH needs an underlying predictive algorithm that learns over time as new change, incident and server data become available, we were not able to leverage these techniques.

(b) Access Restrictions: We had certain data access restrictions across different geographies, which meant that we may not have access to historical change descriptions at risk calculation time to compare them to our incoming change description. As COACH needs to be available to any client account, the data access restriction further limited the selection of machine learning algorithms to a small set. With the change features available to us at change creation time, it was not possible to create a meaningful predictive model through machine learning algorithms.

B. Determining Potential Predictors

Next, we defined a set of potential predictors, based on the different pieces of information available to us at change creation time. We used IBM SPSS Statistics software to perform Chi-square tests on the potential predictors to see if the perceived relationship between the predictors and the change closure code (successful or problematic) is due to chance, or if there is a true association between the

**Table 3** Summary of accuracies for all approaches

| Factor | Test cases = 100 (with 5 results) | Test cases = 100 (with 4 results) | Test cases = 100 (with 3 results) | % of Top result correct |
|---|---|---|---|---|
| Time | 52% | 45% | 42% | 30% |
| All | 67% | 64% | 61% | 51% |
| Significant | 75% | 71% | 70% | 58% |

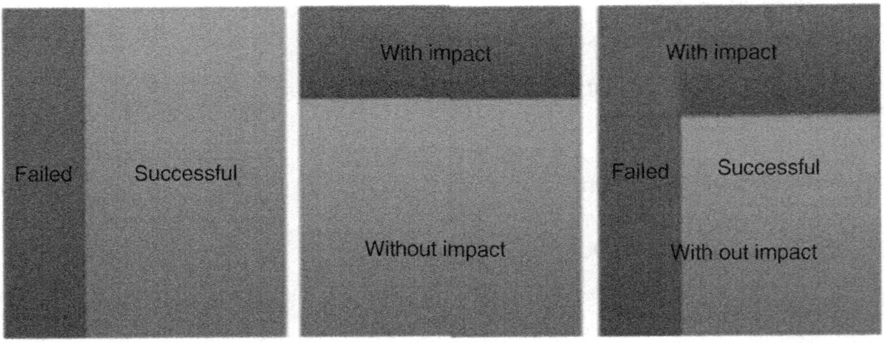


**Fig. 5** Data set for (**a**) Model 1, (**b**) Model 2, (**c**) Model 3

predictors and the outcomes. For example, when we tested the effect of survey risk on change outcome, the p-value = .000 indicated that there's a 0% chance to find the observed (or a larger) degree of association between the variables if they're perfectly independent in the population. In other words, survey risk significantly impacts the change outcome, and thus, is an important predictor for change risk. Similarly, we tested several other predictors using the same method. In the next few sub-sections, we only report on those predictors which were observed to have a strong association (p = .000.) to the outcome (change closure code).

C. Predictor: Risk Assessment Survey

A risk assessment survey typically comprises Probability and Impact questions. For example: How many times have you implemented this type of change? How complex is the implementation? What is the potential business impact in case of failure? Each question is rated, for example, from 1 (the highest) to 5 (the lowest) by the Change Analyst, and the probability and impact values are aggregated through a formula to calculate the final risk through a look-up of a risk matrix.

D. Predictor: Change Failure Rate

In order to calculate change failure rates, we rely on at least one-years' worth of historical data from our data warehouse, which comprises 160 client accounts' operational IT data. By considering a fine-grained change category (see Section II B) and change closure code (successful, failed, issues, backed-out), we can compute the percentage of failed changes in each category. Our definition of a "failed change" comprises any change with {failed, issues, backed-out} closure codes.

E. Predictor: Change Incident Rate

If change closure codes readily indicated whether a change led to an incident, we could have used the same logic as in Section III D to calculate the percentage of changes that cause incidents. Unfortunately, this is usually not the case as it may not be apparent at change closure time whether the change caused an incident, and if it becomes apparent a while later through root cause analysis, it is not practical for

Change Implementers to go back and update closed change records due to time constraints. Instead, we rely on COACH's Change–Incident Link Discovery analytics [7] to mine such change – incident relationships. Once we have the change – incident pairs, we compute what percentage of changes cause incidents in each change category. Our definition of "changes that cause incidents" comprises any change that led to incident(s) and has one of {successful, failed, issues, backed-out} closure codes.

F. Predictor: Server Failure Rate and Server Properties

Server failure rates are important to consider when predicting change risk as they indicate how likely it is that the change running on a server may fail due to the server's current health issues. Server failure rates are determined by statistical modeling and simulation techniques used to study server incidents, utilization, and configurations to classify them into two groups: problematic and non-problematic. Moreover, the simulation component of these capabilities proposes improvement actions for problematic servers along with quantifiable benefits for each (what-if scenarios) [5].

Server properties, such as operating system, manufacturer, environment (production vs. development) are also available to us through our client account data warehouse and will be used to model similar server behavior when we do not have explicit knowledge about the server on which a change would be implemented.

With our predictors identified and confirmed, we can now design a predictive algorithm to calculate change risk based on survey risk, change failure rate, change incident rate and predicted server failure rate.

G. Formalizing Change Risk Prediction Algorithm

Our risk prediction approach takes survey_risk as its basis and provides an adjustment function to increase or lower the risk as determined by COACH. The reason behind this design decision was to leverage the effectiveness of the survey_risk on successful changes to avoid over predicting the actual risk.

## *Differentiation*

**Establishing linkage** With our approach to establishing linkage between CH and IN, in 75% of the time, the correct change causing a given incident appeared in the top five, and in 58% of the time, the top ranking change was the change causing the incident.

The KS-Statistics revealed that only OwnerGroup and NumberofCommonWords dimensions were significant. Based on this premise, we excluded all other dimensions and repeated our test of 100 incidents. We then ranked the changes by confidence and compared them against the ground truth. The results are depicted in Table 3.

**Predicting Problematic change** Table 4 shows accuracy and recall for Predictive Model Targeting Classification of Problematic vs. Non-Problematic Changes.

Our final predictive model yielded an overall accuracy of 84% and 100% recall for correctly identifying any type of failed change (incident causing or not) as problematic. Although the proactive detection of successful changes that led to an incident was lower than for the second predictive model, it is still much higher than the traditional approach (36% vs. 55%). If we consider the performance of all three algorithms in terms of catching problematic changes (failed or successful with incident), we also see that the third model outperforms the rest significantly at 85% coverage. Our work on prevention of change induced incidents is by no means complete, but this analysis sheds some light on the important characteristics of changes to guide future direction.

**COACH** Unlike traditional change risk calculators, our risk prediction is cognitive: it understands the change, learns from a dynamic data set and outcomes, and reasons with a data-driven statistical approach.

An important differentiator of COACH is its ability to provide an all-encompassing risk context in addition to the predicted risk score. It provides different risk dimensions, as well as a comparison of the proposed change's risk to similar changes across all client accounts in our data warehouse. This gives the Change Analyst additional insights regarding what the risk is related to (failure vs. incident, etc.), how the changes belonging to the same change category typically perform within the Change Analyst's account, as well as how the account's performance compares to other accounts for this type of change. The predicted risks are stored and periodically compared against the observed outcomes. While the predictive algorithm itself will adapt over time based on newly observed change outcomes, it is critical to learn additional more fine-grained context from recent inaccurate risk assessments. In order to do so, the predictive algorithm is complemented by looking at the predicted and observed outcome for similar changes in the same change category. If the algorithm predicts a low risk for a change, but a very similar change with a low predicted risk ended up having a problematic outcome, the assessed risk for the change is increased.

Our predictive algorithm provides a significant improvement in our ability to proactively detect problematic changes (0–78%), at the expense of increased false positives (0%–38% high risk for successful changes). We argue that successful changes end up being successful due to correct actions having been taken at change preparation time. This means that 38% of the successful changes can be inherently

**Table 4** Summary of accuracies for all approaches

| | | Failed | | Successful | |
|---|---|---|---|---|---|
| Target | Overall accuracy | With incident | W/O incident | With incident | W/O incident |
| Problematic vs. non problematic | 84% | 100% | 100% | 55% | 89% |

risky but ended up being successful due to the risk being mitigated, and thus our prediction has the potential of being even more accurate than results depicted in Table 5.

## *Change Action Identification*

**Change management process and technology** A change request initiates the change management process. Typically, a change request is documented as a request ticket submitted to a change management ticketing system. The ticket is classified based on its intent and types of change and routed to a specialized sysops group. Before dispatching a work order for the change, the request undergoes an approval process under which the change requestor's access permission, the nature of the target endpoint of the change (e.g., a billing database server) and the type of change to be done (e.g., restart) are scrutinized against a list of business operation policies and security policies. The outcome of the approval process generally falls under:

- reject request due to risk or insufficient permission,
- schedule change against a change window (a period of agreed upon time during which the IT infrastructure of a business client performs batched changes),
- or approved for immediate execution.

A work order is then dispatched either against a sysops group for manual change or against a system automation solution that would automate the change.

**Change request taxonomy** Specialized sysops groups are organized based on change type or technology silos depending on the IT support structure of a business client. For instance, some IT support teams are organized based on skill expertise aligned with specific operation systems (e.g., Linux, Windows, Mainframe, etc.) or specific application types (e.g., DB2, Oracle, MSSQL, etc.). These teams are also loosely aligned with a group or category of IT services (e.g., hardware, software, network, security, etc.). Accordingly, we created a standardized multi-tier taxonomy that reflects the different organization alignments and how different change actions can be categorized within the taxonomy. Our taxonomy follows a top-down

**Table 5** Comparison of survey risk (top) and Predicted risk (bottom) performance

| Survey risk | Successful recall | Problematic recall |
|---|---|---|
| Low | 48% | 12% |
| Med | 52% | 88% |
| High | 0% | 0% |
| Predicated risk | Successful recall | Problematic recall |
| Low | 30% | 8% |
| Med | 32% | 14% |
| High | 38% | 78% |

categorization of: category, task group and action (CTA). Category is a standardized set of top-level IT change service types that are commonly found across all clients: software, hardware, network, security, facility, storage, etc. Task groups are client-specific groupings of similar actions according to the client's IT team organization and distribution of change actions. Typically, a task group addresses a group of similar change actions under a common category (e.g., database maintenance, database backup and restore, etc.). Actions are self-contained change actions that are performed according to a procedure by a sysop or an automation automata/service. Table 6 illustrates some examples of how a change request is mapped to the CTA taxonomy. We further augment the CTA taxonomy with two technology properties, application type (e.g., DB2) and system type (e.g., Linux Redhat). The technology augmentations are necessary as some client's sysop teams are aligned by technology skill proficiency and many automation offerings have specific application and technology dependencies. We purposefully kept the taxonomy structure itself to be technology neutral as we want to focus on the intent of the actions rather than the technologies involved and technologies evolve at a much more rapid pace compared with the changes to the list of actions.

**Change automation** Change automation technology is crucial in supporting AI Driven IT service management as it is after all the action arm of an intelligent process. Any decision making, diagnostics and planning generally result in the need to perform sets of actions. Therefore, it is important to understand how automation solutions are designed and are intended to operate. In the change management context, automations are created as sets of services that can perform specific actions (e.g., create a DB2 database on a Linux server). These services or offerings are generally defined through APIs with accompanying descriptions and parameter requirements. These APIs are created for an integration design purpose, in that the service expects a human designer to understand the intent of the service and ensure the parameters are understood and provided accordingly; it also expects the invocation to these APIs to be performed by another system. Modern self-service change management processes facilitate this invocation by providing a Web-based self-service portal that exposes the list of service/offerings as a catalog and acquire the parameters for the execution via form filling. Validation on the parameter values are performed by checking the types of the value and their consistency against a known system and application relational database (CMDB: configuration management database). There is no established mechanism of mapping a change request description to a automation offering in a catalog.

**Action identification challenges** To quantify the coverage of service automation catalogs against a specific set of client's change request, we need to perform action identification from change request tickets from natural-language description of the requests themselves. Several non-trivial challenges need to be dealt with: the set of unstructured texts are large (tens of millions) and service offering catalogs are rather large (thousands of actions); IT change request descriptions are often ill-formed, short texts with domain-specific acronyms and non-English keywords; action and

**Table 6** Examples of change request classification to category, task and action

| Change requests | Category | Task | Actions |
|---|---|---|---|
| *Create new X database on instance Y.* | Database | Management | Create DB |
| *Enable user X on Y database.* | Database | User admin | Grant user |
| *Stop DB2 database on X PROD server: Y.* | Database | Run operations | Stop DB |
| *Increase CPU for X to 8vcpu.* | Hardware | cpu | Increase cpu |

noun variances between ticket description and offerings are very high; and action words have very different semantics depending on specific categories.

**Natural-Language classification and action identification** We have conducted a series of research and experimentation on ticket classification [14] and NL-based intent identification [15]. Natural-language classification (NLC) is relied on for identifying intent of a service request and mapping it to a known offering catalog. We have structured the offerings in the catalogs according to the CTA taxonomy. However, to deal with the challenges, we still need to find a scalable way of creating a knowledge base of IT change action intents, handle linguistic variances of IT service management terminologies, concepts and technology utterances, and finally be able to perform natural-language classification on short request descriptions. To this end, we applied topic modeling and deep learning to be able to generate representative symptoms from short text descriptions. We then applied a transfer learning technique to create knowledge that could account for a large amount of ITSM terminologies and category-specific variances. The knowledge on valid category-action-noun associations that we mined can then be used as feedback to further improve the NLC process. Figure 6 illustrates the change request action identification and mapping process.

**Differentiation** Topic modeling and clustering techniques such as frequency-based clustering, Latent Dirichlet Allocation (LDA), Non-negative Matrix Factorization (NMF) and Autoencoders help us to identify clusters of verbs and nouns and their common occurrences. The knowledge gained from the clustering process helps to expand our knowledge base that is applicable across clients. Through community detection, we further assign the clusters to categories (the top-level classification of our CTA taxonomy). Valid action pairs (verb-noun association) from the clusters are then generated by both filtering them through our knowledge base as well as by examining their relevance and co-occurrence within the change request ticket dataset and matching them to the service offering descriptions. The outcome is a training set of labelled requests associated with category-action labels used to train NLC classifiers. We have experimented with rule-based classifiers, Watson NLC and Passive-aggressive classifiers (PAC). Figure 7 shows an example of how verb and noun identification from requests are performed and how a knowledge graph is used to create the entity relations needed for rule-generation.

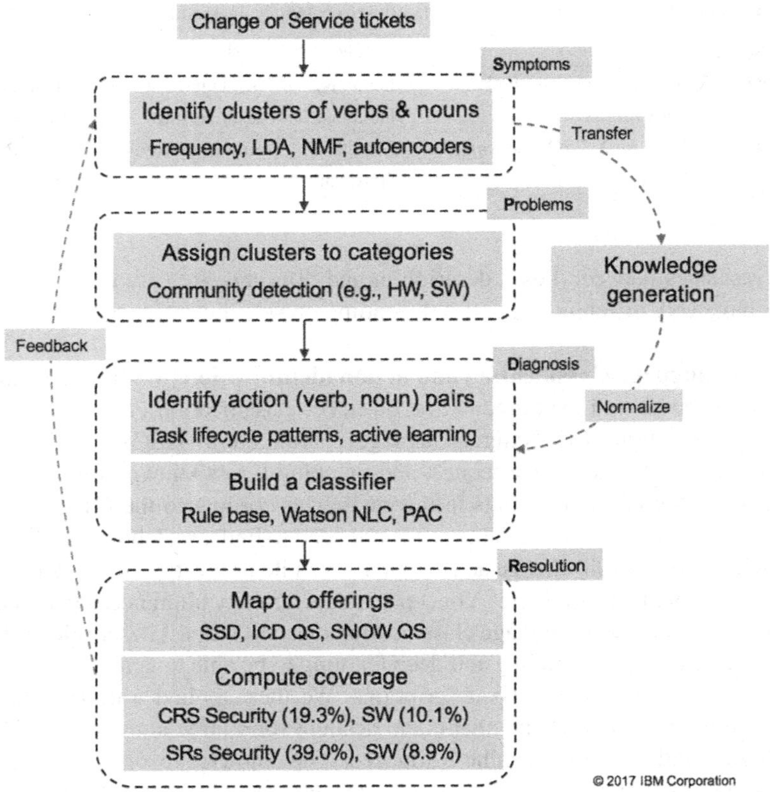


**Fig. 6** Change request action identification and catalog mapping

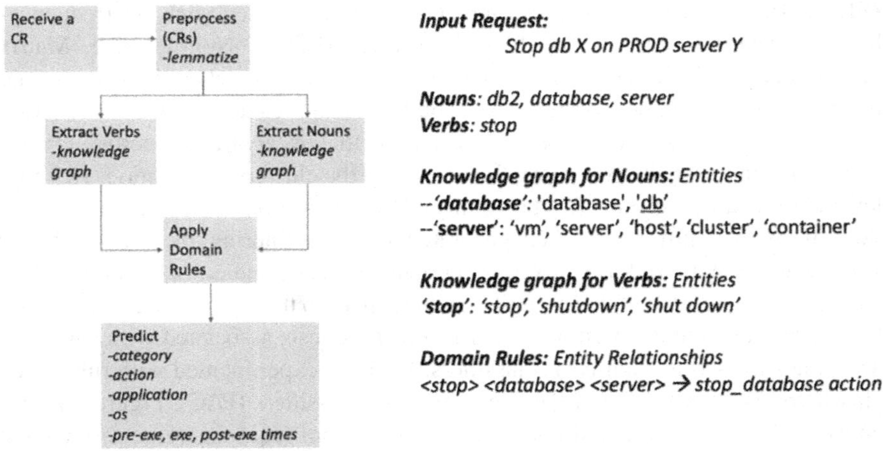


**Fig. 7** Example of verb and noun identification and rule generation

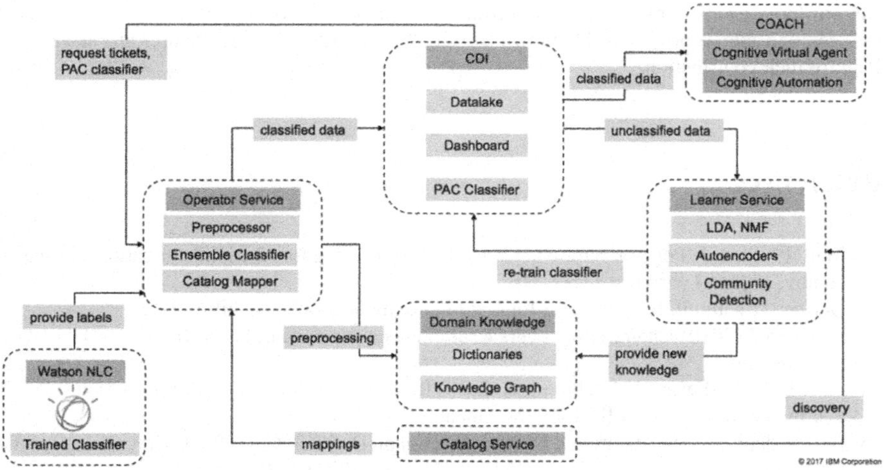


**Fig. 8** Transfer learning and knowledge generation process

Figure 8 illustrates the transfer learning process we used to generate the knowledge base. Unclassified data from a ticket source (i.e., unclassified change request tickets) are fed into the learner process that performs the verb-noun identification and request clustering. This in turn expands our knowledge base and improves the classifiers. The classifiers (operator service) are then used to operate on new change request tickets to provide classification and mapping to catalog offerings, and any unclassified requests then go through the learning process as feedbacks.

## Dataset Description

Our dataset is assembled from real client account data, and comprises 1600 changes, 50% of which are used for training and the remaining 50% for testing.

## Conclusion and Future Work

We continue to explore techniques that will help transfer knowledge and adapt trained models when new client's requests are on-boarded. Our initial investigations suggest that action-noun based approach scales better than conventional NL-based classifiers, however further evaluation and experimentation is needed. Moreover, we will attempt to extend our approach to non-English languages, starting with French, Spanish and German.

Additional details of methodology described in this chapter can be found in [11–13].

**Acknowledgements** This work was done through collaboration of IBM Research and Technical services, and authors are grateful to Sinem Guven, Karin Murthy, Jin Xiao, Anup Kalia and Sander Plug for their contribution.

## References

1. Mairal J, Bach F, Ponce J, Sapiro G (2010) Online learning for matrix factorization and sparse coding. J Mach Learn Res 11:19–60
2. Gartner IT summit, best practices for continuous application availability, 2005.
3. Druebert J (2010) Changes, incidents & unintended consequences. In: Insight on IT service management
4. Tang L, Li T, Shwartz L, Grabarnik G (2013) Recommending resolutions for problems identified by monitoring. In: IFIP/IEEE IM, Ghent
5. Bogojeska J, Lanyi D, Giurgiu I, Stark G, Wiesmann D (2013) Classifying server behavior and predicting impact of modernization actions. In: IFIP/IEEE CNSM, Zurich
6. Agarwal S, Sindhgatta R, Sengupta B (2012) SmartDispatch: enabling efficient ticket dispatch in an IT service environment. In: ACM KDD, Beijing
7. Güven S, Barbu C, Husemann D, Wiesmann D (2012) Change risk expert. In: IFIP/IEEE NOMS, Maui, HI
8. Hagen S, Seibold M, Kemper A (2012) Efficient verification of IT change. In: IFIP/IEEE NOMS, Maui, HI
9. Lipitakis A-D, Kotsiantis S (2014) A hybrid Machine Learning methodology for imbalanced datasets. In: IEEE IISA, Crete
10. Bulut F (2016) Performance evaluations of supervised learners on imbalanced datasets. In: Electric Electronics, Computer Science, Biomedical Engineerings' Meeting (EBBT)
11. Güven S, Murthy K (2016) Understanding the role of change in incident prevention. In: IEEE/IFIP CNSM, Montreal
12. Güven S, Murthy K, Shwartz L, Paradkar A (2016) Towards establishing causality between Change and Incident. IEEE/IFIP NOMS, Turkey
13. Güven S, Jasionowski P, Murthy K, Tunga K, Stark G (2017) COACH: COgnitive Analytics for CHange. IEEE/IFIP IMS, Portugal
14. Kalia A, Xiao J, Bulut M, Vukovic M, Anerousis N (2017) Cataloger: catalog recommendation service for IT change requests. In: ICSOC, Spain
15. Kalia A, Telang P, Xiao J, Vukovic M (2017) Quark: a methodology to transform people-driven processes to chatbot services. In: ICSOC, Spain

# AI for Solution Design

## Background

Before we explain how AI could be leveraged to dramatically transform the "Solutioning" phase, it is important to outline the role of this phase across the Service Delivery lifecycle as well as the major personas involved.

As illustrated in Fig. 1, the goal of the Solution Design phase is to design and assemble the final IT solution based on the discussions and requirements gathered in the "Advisory" phase; the outcome the Solution Design phase will then feed the "Build" phase where the solution is actually built and inserted in the client's IT landscape and the "Operate" phase where the designed solution is put in production and operated according to the agreed SLAs.

Some key personas mentioned below are relevant for the Solutioning phase:

- The Technical Solution Manager ("Adam") is responsible for mapping client requirements and baselines (volumes) into a complete solution and ensuring the right price point is met
- The domain Subject Matter Expert ("Jeremy") is in charge of defining architectural patterns, blueprints, and best practices for his own specific domain (e.g. Storage, Network, Change Mgmt., …). Jeremy also acts as primary "information source" for Adam during solution definition.
- The Client provides requirements (generally in textual documents)

Figure 2 describes the steps that are traditionally taken during the Solution Design phase in the Service Provider Industry. It is worth noting that while the described steps pertain to IT Service Delivery, a similar process is found for delivery of services in other industries, e.g. the construction industry.

The process is typically initiated by the client issuing a "Request for Proposal" (RFP) accompanied by a set of documents which contain the client's point of view concerning the IT services to be provided as well as the detailed requirements



K. Kloeckner et al., *Transforming the IT Services Lifecycle with AI Technologies*, SpringerBriefs in Computer Science,
https://doi.org/10.1007/978-3-319-94048-9_4

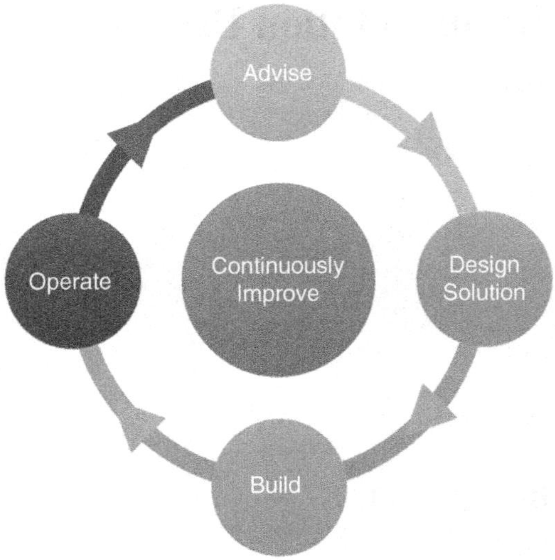


**Fig. 1** Service delivery lifecycle

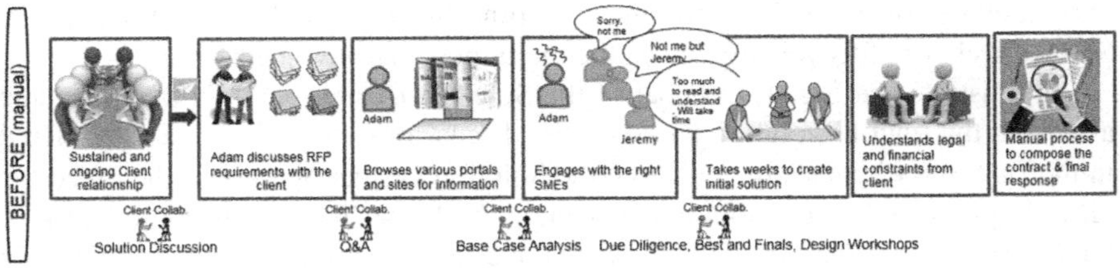


**Fig. 2** Current steps and actors in the Solutioning today

(functional and nonfunctional, i.e. constraints) that must characterize the solution itself. The information contained in these documents is largely unstructured and quite often needs a lot of clarifications in a quite long convergence process.

In a subsequent step, Adam, the Technical Solution Manager searches for relevant information on the provider's service delivery capabilities to fulfill the client's requirements. This step relies a lot on tacit knowledge that is scattered, neither codified not mapped. In most cases, success depends on the skill of the individual practitioner and/or on her ability to connect with the relevant players and SMEs. Moreover, the solution design suffers from a lack of data-driven evidence and references to similar solutions that are already in the Operate phase of the life cycle.

In addition to solution creation depending on the individual's knowledge and network, tool support is fragmented and disconnected. As a result, process execution is very waterfall and sequential. Issues or changes requested by clients in at one step generally require a "back to square one". This greatly limits true innovation in the arrangement of the solution (tradeoff assessments, what-if analysis, optimization) and severely inhibits the degree of collaboration or even co-creation with the client himself.

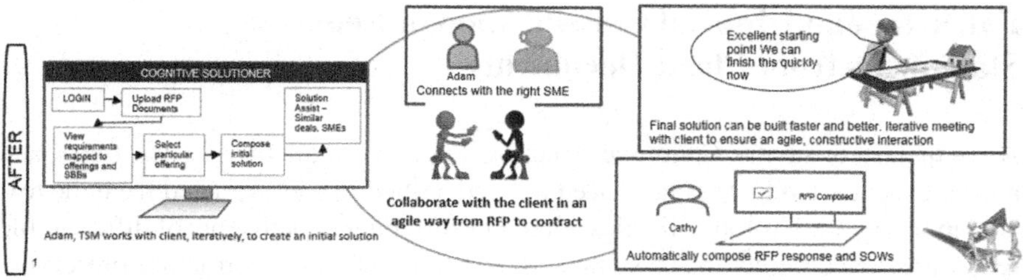


**Fig. 3** The optimized state enabled with the Cognitive Solution Designer

Applying AI technologies helps to fundamentally transform this process and to overcome the described challenges. The "Cognitive Solution Designer" tool (CogSol) enables Adam, the Technical Solution Manager, to collaborate with the client in an agile way from RFP to solution and contract (Fig. 3).

In particular, the new process enables:

- **Speed and business agility:** The entire flow is basically now transformed into a set of micro-feedback loops that build one on top of the other along a very agile construct. This ultimately leads to shorter solutioning times and a far better way to adjust to sudden and unexpected business conditions (eg. new requirements, security threats, etc.).
- **Continuous collaboration across the major parties and stakeholders:** Every persona (e.g. the solutioner, the architect, the client, …) has the right context to collaborate and contribute; iteration and innovation are fostered and supported by the Cognitive Solutioning Knowledge base.
- **Continuous learning:** The system is constantly learning; for example, the knowledge acquired in previous engagements makes the system perform better in following iterations. In this way, the huge set of data available in IBM, for example architectural blueprints, solution building blocks, data coming from the universe of client implementations etc. could be fully harvested for new solutions.
- **Social curation:** We assert that it is critical to truly leverage the technical community as "social curator" of the entire Cognitive Solutioning Knowledge base to be able to capitalize on the important expertise and 'real life' experience that every practitioner is gathering every single day and that would be otherwise lost or relegated to scattered and anecdotal conversations.
- **Client co-creation and intimacy:** We have observed that the benefits coming from the Cognitive Solutioning approach go well beyond merely the Solutioning phase and are completely changing the game in terms of client relationship as well. This allows a true co-creation with the client and a deeper level of interaction and understanding of the client landscape.

In the following we describe in detail the technical challenges and their AI-based solution in the Cognitive Solution Designer Tool.

## Extraction and Topical Classification of Requirement Statements from Client Documents

As a first step, in the Cognitive Solution Designer tool, the service types and attributes requested by the client need to be identified in and extracted from the text documents as well as topically classified. For this, client documents of different file types are loaded into the system and transformed into a structure-preserving sentence-level representation for extraction, i.e. for each sentence its association with a subsection, section or list is preserved. Subsequently, functional requirements ("which services?"), nonfunctional requirements ("under which constraint?") and baselines ("volumes for the service") are extracted and topically categorized.

## Challenge

The accuracy of the proposed solution critically depends on the initial requirements extraction step and topical classification step: a mediocre level of accuracy not only negatively affects the downstream solutioning process but it also diminishes the confidence of the practitioner.

**Challenge 1** Identification and extraction of sentences containing requirements. Typically, the client requirements are distributed over tens of RFP documents mixed with descriptions of the client's current IT landscape, details about the RFP response process the prospective provider needs to follow, as well as details on contractual terms and conditions. Table 1 contains example sentences from real RFP documents, where the first three sentences contain technical requirements while the second three do not. The example illustrates that no simple method that e.g. would identify certain independent verbs or modal verbs would be highly accurate.

**Table 1** Example sentences from RFP documents

| |
|---|
| The client looks to the service provider to perform all remote operations services, such as common software image development, anti-virus, patch management and other associated services. |
| Provide requirements for high-level dashboard performance monitoring, including real-time and historical analysis |
| Establish system monitoring thresholds (e.g., utilization, capacity) to track data center system components (servers, storage, databases, etc.) performance in accordance with service levels |
| The client expects the supplier to provide a realistic approach to meeting the timeline, and will be evaluated on their ability to execute that approach. |
| Collaborative computing services are the activities associated with supporting collaborative tools (e.g., MS exchange/outlook). |
| All RFP responses must be provided no later than the date and time specified in Table x. |

**Challenge 2** Topical classification of requirement statements. In order to identify matching service capabilities, the extracted requirements statements need to be topically classified. Several aspects make this classification problem especially challenging, yet it is expected that this challenge is present in many requirement-to-delivery capability matching scenarios. First of all, to match the appropriate capability to the requirement we need fine-grained classes. In particular, we have about 20 classes at the first level, e.g. "Enterprise Security", and about 300 classes across the first and second categorization levels, e.g. "Enterprise Security – Identity and Access". Consequently, large numbers of training data are needed for any supervised classification approach. However, unlike in other domains, like movie sentiment classification or labeling of pictures, such training data did not exist prior to this effort. Training data needs to be created for the purpose of the project and involves a massive labeling effort. Third, classification of a sentence or a functional requirement needs to be done in the context of a paragraph, subsection, or list, as the information contained in the statement itself sometimes proves to be insufficient.

## Solution Overview

**Identification and extraction of sentences containing requirements** As mentioned in the challenge section, identification of requirements merely based on the choice of independent verbs is insufficient. However, verbs do contain a strong differentiation between requests and definitions and descriptions. Consequently, we follow the identification approach described in [1]: identification of sentences with (1) verbs indicative of a request for service and (2) learned linguistic features for refinement. A third step to the approach in [1] was added comprising a final filtering using binary classifier to reduce false positive identification.

Step (1) is solely based on a positively-labeled set of sentences, i.e. sentences containing requirements statements. From these data sets, we determine the independent verbs and store them as <responsibility verb|true>. If a verb encloses other verbs, it is stored as <responsibility verb|false> unless there exists at least one instance of the verb as independent in which case it is stored as <responsibility verb|true>. This algorithm creates an inclusive set of responsibility verbs, i.e. a sentence containing a responsibility verb is a necessary but not sufficient condition for it being identified as a requirement sentence.

In the second step, the linguistic features indicative of requirements are learned. The training set contains all labeled sentences with responsibility verbs. Feature candidates consist of ordered sequences of POS tags, semantic role features of the verb of interest [2], and language token types. It is immediately clear, that a feature space created in this manner is very large and sparse. Thus we have chosen a Winnow classifier which is theoretically guaranteed to quickly converge to a correct hypothesis in a setting with many irrelevant features, no label noise, and a linear separation of the classes [3]. It belongs to the family of online learning algorithms thus also enabling immediate updates from feedback.

In the third and final step, we prune false positives from the requirement candidate set. The majority of such false positive identifications are requirement statements which do not pertain to a requested technical service but to the way the service provider needs to submit the offer, e.g. the last statement in Table 1 They use a similar set of independent verbs and have a similar structure and will thus be identified as requirements in steps 1 and 2. Yet they are irrelevant for selecting the correct technical capability for the solution. We have found that training a final binary classifier e.g. gradient boosting machine on bag of word representation of the section title is most efficient and effective to distinguish technical from process requirements.

Table 2 shows the results for the trained extraction method tested on three documents with a total of 810 sentences, out of which 68% contained requirements.

**Topical classification of requirement statements:**

To address these difficulties, our approach contains the following elements:

1. To bootstrap the classification, together with senior SMEs, we developed a lexicon with single keywords and multi-word key phrases for all classes in the 2-level class hierarchy. In the initial version of the tool, sentences were classified using this lexicon and by applying a rich set of rules to evaluate position-based occurrence of the lexicon key phrases with the learned weights for these rules.
2. To continuously improve the accuracy, we enable the user to add/remove/change tool-identified requirements and their classifications and thus provide feedback on the tool-generated classification. These manual corrections serve the immediate purpose of correcting the identified requirements for the RFP documents in process. The corrected and validated set will subsequently be used to select the matching service capabilities. At the same time, the user feedback generates new training samples to build a training data set sufficient for supervised classifiers and improve the accuracy.
3. To boost the user experienced accuracy and focus the user feedback in an active-learning manner, similar to [4], we leave sentences unclassified where classification confidence is low.
4. To switch from a manually-created and maintained lexicon we evaluated a number of supervised machine learning methods and found convolutional neural networks (CNNs) to perform better than additive tree models (ATM) training using a bag of words (BOW) representation in the domain embedding space even with smaller training data sets.
5. As discussed, in some cases, the information contained in the sentence itself is insufficient to yield an accurate enough classification. If the confidence is below a threshold, the classification of surrounding sentences belonging to the same subsection as well as that of the subsection title is taken into account. This approach leverages the structure-preserving parsing of incoming documents. All parameters of this approach are optimized during the model selection phase.

**Table 2** Precision and Recall for Requirement Extraction

| Precision | Recall |
|---|---|
| 0.84 | 0.85 |

Figure 4 shows a comparison of the precision and recall for the six most important first-level classes achieved with the lexicon-based classification compared to the convolutional neural network based classification after growing the training set to 4500 labeled instances for all first-level classes. For recall, the CNN approach outperforms for all six classes, indicating the much richer representation of class essence beyond keywords and key phrases. For precision, the CNN based classifier performs better or equal for five out of the six classes.

Figure 5 shows the learning curves for three selected classes. As can be immediately seen, the scope and (thus) variance of textual representations belonging to a class differ dramatically between classes and thus the training data needs to reach sufficient precision and recall. For instance, for Class 1, a little over 200 labeled training sample are sufficient to reach high precision and recall (>90%), while yielding much lower precision and recall for the other two classes. In addition to discovering the level of training needs, we can also observe two other effects: (a) training data covering only a subset of the class and (b) noisy training data. The latter effect can be observed for Class 5, where recall reaches about 90%, yet, the precision is low and stagnant, indicating a noisy training data set. We will further discuss the approaches to clean ground-truth data sets to reduce the labeling noise in the continuous learning on the job deployment in the solution to the third challenge.

## *Differentiation*

For the requirements extraction and classification, we strongly focused on creating a viable first version and learning on the job. To this end, the first deployed instances of the tool could be partly based on applying rules for extraction and classification.

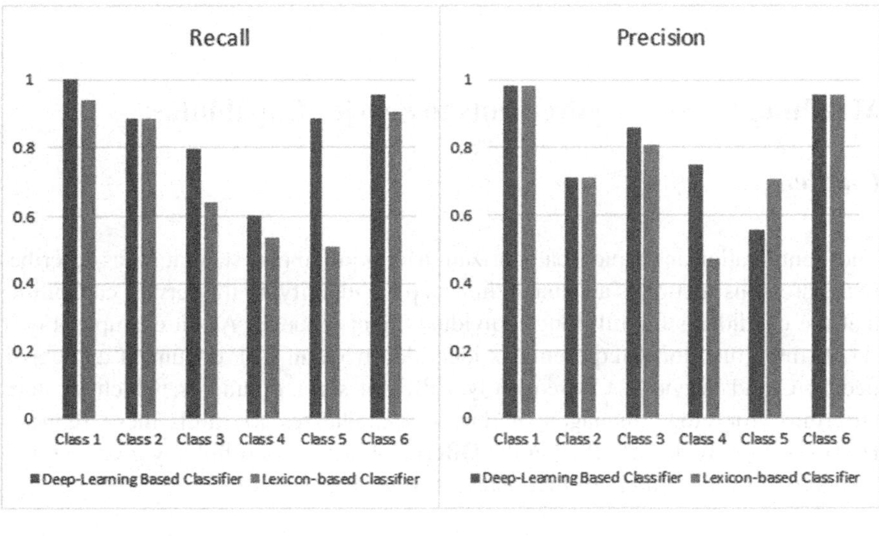


**Fig. 4** Comparison of precision and recall

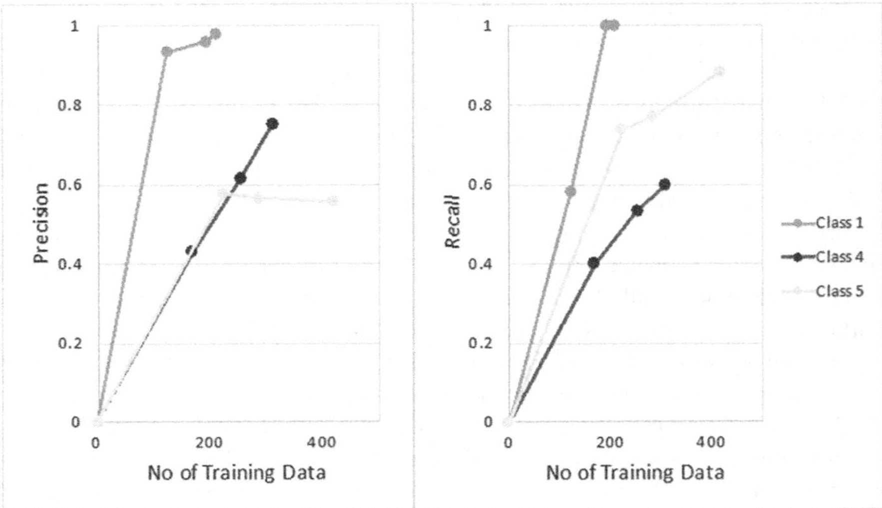


**Fig. 5** Learning curves for selected classes

Yet, even in the very first version, the user would be guided to perform selected corrections with the dual purpose of creating a validated set of requirements for the downstream solution creation *and* the creation of a larger training set. As soon as the training set becomes large enough to yield sufficient performance with supervised methods, these could be put into the field and trained directly from subsequent user feedback for continuous improvement. In our view, the pragmatic combination of rule/regular expression based methods and best in class neural network algorithms allows to overcome the initial lack of training data and excessive cost of dedicated label creation.

## Matching Client Requirements to Service Capabilities

### *Challenge*

The identification and topical categorization of requirements statements as described in the previous section is a valuable first step for identifying the service capabilities that are candidates for fulfilling individual client requests. As an example, Fig. 6 shows three functional requirements identified from an RFP document and classified as Cloud Services. Consequently, different service bundles, which we term Offerings, for cloud management become candidates to fulfill these requests. However, to truly decide whether the Offering capabilities fulfill any given requirements in this topical area, further analysis is needed.

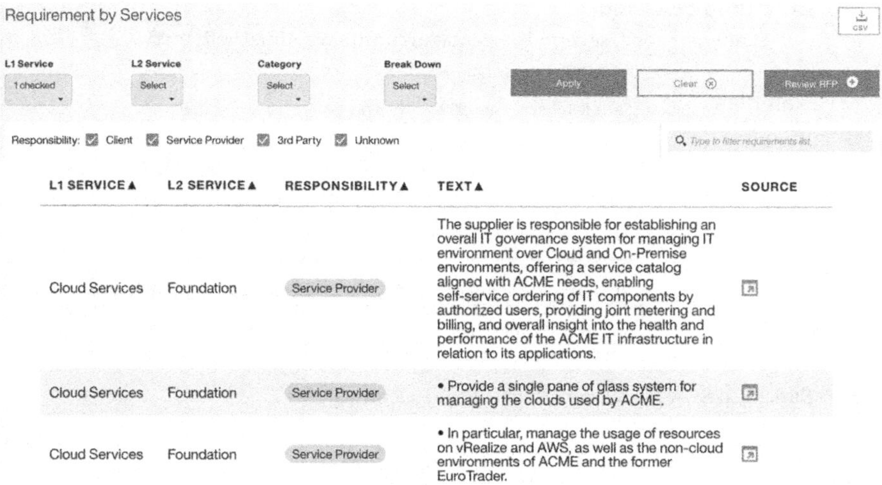


**Fig. 6** Identified and topically categorized functional requirements

## *Solution Overview*

To achieve a deeper comparison between client requests and service capabilities bundled in Offerings, we further distinguish between two types of requirements: (1) functional requirements, i.e. "what" types of services are requested, and (2) non-functional requirements, i.e. "how" these services should be delivered. Nonfunctional requirements include constraints like regulations and delivery countries and design points like service level agreements on availability or resolution times for issues. While the textual and conceptual representation of the functional requirements is varied and complex, nonfunctional requirements can be described through fewer concepts and thus lend themselves to a structured representation.

In Fig. 7 we show the structured representation for service level agreements together with three example statements. Once such structured representations are created for the client's non-functional requirements and – if not available already – in the same manner for the service capabilities, it becomes straightforward to assess the compatibility of the capabilities with the request. For an SLA, type needs to be identical, scope of the capabilities needs to include scope of the request, and percentage of availability of the service capability needs to exceed that of the request, while response time capability needs to be lower than that in the request. Synonyms, hyponyms, and hypernyms for type and scope can be taken into account during the reasoning and/or the extraction into the structured format to make the comparison less dependent on the choice of words.

In the following we first describe the methods used for the extraction of nonfunctional requirements into structured representations for a deeper comparison

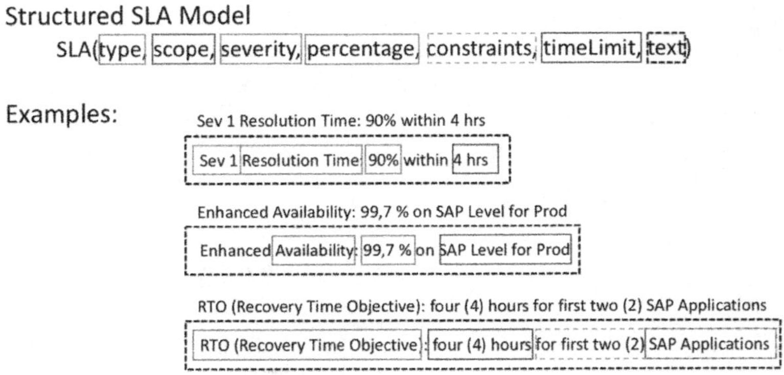


**Fig. 7** Structured SLA Model and example SLA statements

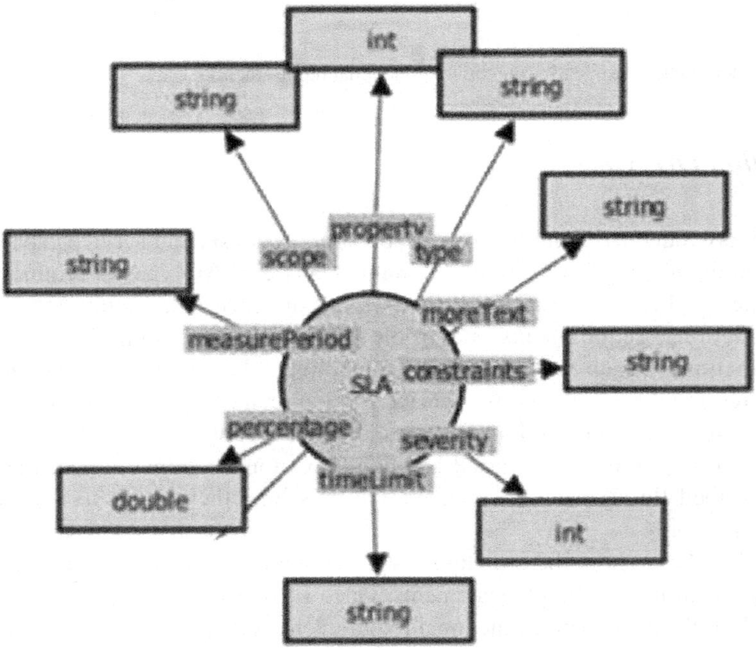


**Fig. 8** Ontology for service level agreements

described above. Subsequently, we discuss solutions to the open questions around deeper comparisons for functional requirements.

There is a wide range of literature on Software Requirement extraction from natural language that shares a number of commonalities with our problem. We have decided to build on the approach of [5] to parse the non-functional requirements and in particular Service Level Agreements with Ontology-based semantic role labeling. The underlying Ontology is shown in Fig. 8. As in [5], in the first step, we instantiate the words in the ontology concepts SLA and type. This is followed by the detection of words and phrases that are related to the SLA and type instances. These are subsequently classified into the property class, i.e. scope or severity.

The first step relies largely on the word forms and work lemmata as well as the POS tag and its word vector, while word forms, POS tag, and dependency between words are most important to identify the other attributes of an SLA.

For the assessment of functional requirements, it is rather infeasible to parse them into an ontology to assess whether the service bundles have the right capabilities. Conceptually, text entailment methods applied to requirement statements from RFPs and capabilities from the service Statements of Work are most promising. However, these are based on training deep neural networks and thus require large amounts of training data that is expensive to create from scratch. We consequently opted for an intermittent step of equipping the user to assess the fit for purpose and while doing so creating training data for future text entailment models. In particular, we plan to determine the most similar capability statement for each extracted functional requirement for visual assessment and user feedback.

### *Differentiation*

Unlike in the case of Software Requirement parsing, requirement statements in the IT Services RFPs – and in other complex service relations e.g. construction – can be very diverse and the underlying concepts very complex. We have thus opted to not attempt a full parsing of both functional and non-functional requirements after extraction and topical classification. Rather we have limited the adoption of SRL for the constraints and design points contained in the non-functional requirements and plan to leverage text entailment models to assess whether capability statements entail, i.e. are compatible with service requests.

## Social Curation and Continuous Learning

### *Challenge*

The actual business value provided by the tool is of course very dependent on the ability of the Cognitive Solution designer tool to effectively capture the requirements and be able to deal with the various nuances that are present in every client driven documentation and that may vary depending on the specific service area or even on the client geography.

**Challenge1** During the early test phases, it became immediately clear that the standard "una tantum" training approach was largely insufficient and we had to augment it with a "continuous learning" mechanism. We needed to make the "learning process" dynamic and continuous so the Cognitive Solution Designer tool can continuously improve and better adapt itself to changing business conditions. In other words, we had to find a way to elevate the "training phase" of the Cognitive Solution designer tool: from being a "one off" phase performed in the lab typically at the beginning of the project to become an integral part of the e2e DevOps process for the tool under the "continuous improvement" cycle.

**Challenge2** Services organizations, like IBM Global Services, are large and have many solution architects, so it is in general very difficult to unify the entire knowledge and expertise of such a technical community. Therefore, the second challenge resides in the ability for Cognitive Solution Designer to have the technical community as primary actor behind the "continuous learning and improvement" cycle – not just for extracting and topically classifying clients' requirements but also to select the best matching offerings and services. In this way, the Cognitive Solution Designer becomes not only a tool to dramatically streamline the solution lifecycle but also a powerful catalyst to federate and organize in a cohesive and machine consumable knowledge base the entire set of service expertise that would have been otherwise scattered and confined just to people heads.

**Challenge3** The great value of the "Social Curation" approach mentioned in the previous challenge may be severely undermined if we do not also include a strong governance system that "accepts" user feedback which will ultimately lead to a better accuracy level for the Cognitive Solution Designer tool and automatically reject annotations that would produce a "quality drift".

## *Solution Overview*

We address the challenges outlined above with three solution concepts: (1) capture user feedback pervasively, (2) design the appropriate incorporation of the user feedback, (3) design methodologies to prevent quality drift through either poor or malicious training feedback.

**Capture feedback pervasively** User feedback is essential to create an ever improving and evolving system. Yet, explicit feedback from users might be hard to motivate if it involves a large effort from the user. Thus, we designed and redesigned our user feedback mechanism aiming at a perfect balance of minimalism and usefulness.

Figure 9 shows a screenshot of the document viewer with the overlaid tool created annotations for the client requirements. It takes just two clicks for the user to

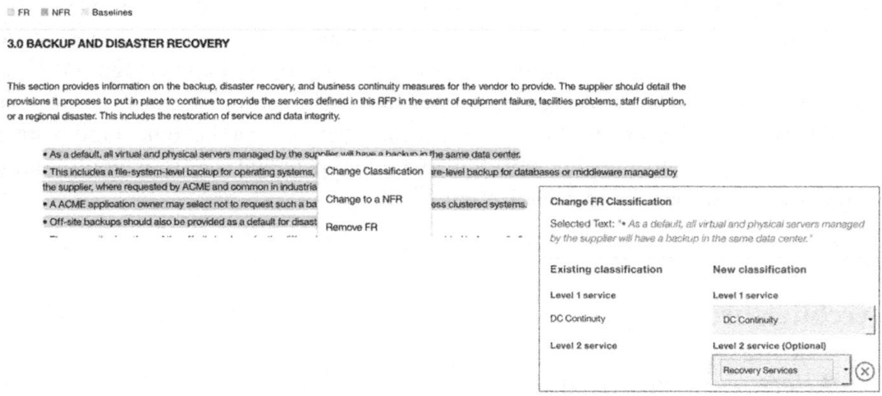


**Fig. 9** Document viewer with text annotations and pop-up window for correcting tool created annotations

correct them for the subsequent matching of requirements and capabilities and each such correction is used as a new training instance for continuous improvement. Similarly, accepted tool extractions and classifications are leveraged as new training examples. Similarly, in the decision trees that request user input to refine the selection of appropriate services with strategic considerations, we allow users to use a comment field to add further considerations based on their experience.

**Continuous learning** The continuous feedback collection described above allows for the continuous improvement/continuous learning in all machine learning and knowledge driven decision support models in the tool. However, the update strategy and learning algorithms depend on the model specifies. For the requirement extraction where we use an online-learning scheme, updates to the machine learning algorithm will be performed incrementally and near-real time. For requirements classification where we use a deep-learning based approach, updates are performed regularly by retraining the network. Going forward, to increase the computational efficiency, we are looking into applying incremental learning approaches that have been recently developed for deep neural networks [7]. Another aspect of continuous learning based on user feedback is the prevention of drift or degradation of the training corpus. Here we are applying and extending existing approaches to clean ground-truth data set [5, Agarwal 2007] to reduce the labeling noise and keep it low in the continuous learning on the job deployment.

## *Differentiation*

The ability to capture "implicit" user feedback (typically monitoring user undo or retries) in order to further tune the underlying engine is today becoming more and more common in AI systems (typically chatbots).

With the "social curation" approach we have implemented for the Cognitive Solution designer tool we have moved one step further: we solicit and incentivize the technical community to contribute and augment the overall knowledge and company expertise in solution design in an open and highly collaborative fashion. This has not only produced better business outcomes, but has also become a motivating factor for the solution architect workforce who find personal reward in contributing to the success of the overall organization.

## Architecture

### *Architectural considerations*

To better understand the architectural choices adopted in CogSol, it is important to outline the key design points that CogSol has to address:

- **Coverage of a quite extensive and broad set of scenarios, personas and "interaction styles".** In fact, as emerged from the various Design Thinking sessions we had at the beginning of the project, the set of user scenarios that CogSol must realize covers a very diverse set of use cases (requirement mapping, solution assembly, data curation, knowledge management, etc.) involving a set of personas with very different goals and professional backgrounds (solution architects, domain subject matter experts, deal manager, etc.)
- **Main realization of the "outer loop" for the entire Platform**. CogSol has been designed not only as a key application that would streamline the entire solutioning phase but also the core component of the "outer Loop" for the entire Platform that would provide "knowledge driven service improvement" capabilities to all the rest of consumable services hosted on the Platform.
- **Data driven approach**. As described above the very large majority of use cases in CogSol rely on data manipulation and transformation (for example ingestion of RFPs / RFS into the system or annotation of data corpus). CogSol must provide a very efficient way to handle these use cases both from a "quality of service" standpoint (e.g. performance, latency, availability, etc.) as well as from a "data semantic" perspective (eg. domain entity recognition, data abstraction, data composition in higher representations, etc.)
- **Knowledge management foundation for the Platform**. CogSol needs to provide the basic primitives in terms of knowledge management for the rest of the Services Platform in terms of knowledge representation, knowledge manipulation and knowledge federation.

Without getting into low level implementation details we now want to describe the major architectural design elements implemented in CogSol that have enabled addressing the above mentioned "design points".

(a) **Upfront definition of major scenario flows** (with links to use cases and key personas) with articulation of the most relevant "interface" points and mapping with key high level architectural components.

As an example the figure below represents the high level view for the key components and services concerning the RFP phase.

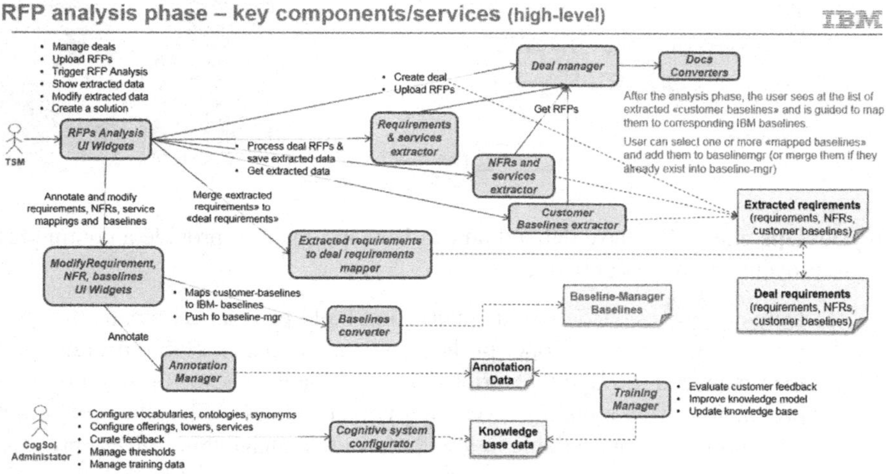


(b) **Adoption of an MVC (Model View Controller pattern) approach based on micro-services.**

- Definition of groups of related micro-services (especially the ones with similar responsibilities and working on adjacent data), together in higher level «services». Assignment of clear responsibilities and APIs to «services»
- Leveraging the Kubernetes framework
- Shielding the details of data-model and data structures through a data service that provides forward compatible REST APIs and data helpers.
- Implementation of a flexible Data service that is a modular component that can be split into different data services that can be used by other components to provide data-persistence and retrieval function in a standard way
- This approach has also enabled lot of reuse of existing components through simple refactoring

The following picture expands the RFP use cases shown above and presents the linkage with "micro-services groups" and data layer.

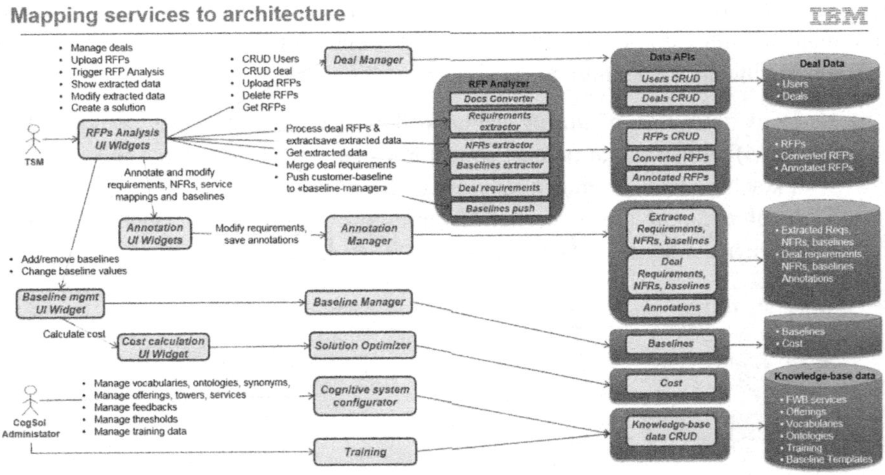


(c) **DevOps chain**. We have defined an e2e DevOps chain to provide a continuous improvement process at two levels:

1. Delivery process: Continuous-integration build process, automatically triggered each time a developer pushes new code into a GitHub repository and then managed through the various DevOps chain stages till promotion into production; we are mainly leveraging UrbanCode as well as the core of the DevOps toolchain available in the Platform to manage this delivery process
2. Continuous knowledge refinement: CogSol is not only a typical aaS application that needs to live on the Platform and leverage the e2e DevOps continuous delivery process just described. CogSol also enables somewhat "continuous delivery and refinement of knowledge "powered by our practitioner community thru the annotation and "social curation" methods described in this paper. This is the reason why we have augmented our DevOps chain to include all the steps and mechanisms needed to keep our CogSol knowledge base always fresh and up to date

## Conclusion

In the "Cognitive Solution Designer" tool, we have developed and applied AI technologies to fundamentally transform the IT Delivery solutioning process to enable speed and agility in understanding the clients' requirements, co-creation of solutions with the client and continuous learning from the practitioners using the system. In order to create such a system, we solved and continue to solve NLP and machine learning challenges from identifying client requirements in large text documents to deep matching of such requirements with service capabilities to establishing efficient and robust continuous learning approaches.

**Acknowledgements** We'd like to thank the whole "Cognitive Solution Designer" research and development team and all visionary supporters of this project.

## References


1. Nezhad HRM, et al. eAssistant: cognitive assistance for identification and auto-triage of actionable conversations. WWW2017.
2. Màrquez L, Carreras X, Litkowski KC, Stevenson S (2008) Semantic role labeling: an introduction to the special issue. Comput Linguist 34(2):145–159
3. Nigam K, Hurst M (2004) Towards a robust metric of opinion. In Proceedings of the AAAI Spring Symposium on Exploring Attitude and Affect in Text: Theories and Applications.
4. Bakis R, Connors DP, Dube P, Kapanipathi P, Kumar A, Malioutov D, Venkatramani C (2017) Performance of natural language classifiers in a question-answering system. IBM J Res Develop 61(4):14:1–14:10
5. Roth M, Klein E ( 2015) Parsing software requirements with an ontology-based semantic role labeler. Proceedings of the 1st Workshop on Language and Ontologies
6. Käding C et al (2016) Fine-tuning deep neural networks in continuous learning scenarios, Asian Conference on Computer Vision. Springer, Cham
7. Sumeet A, et al. (2007) How much noise is too much: A study in automatic text classification. Data Mining, 2007. ICDM 2007. Seventh IEEE International Conference on. IEEE.

# Conversational IT Service Management

## Background

Conversational AI permeates our daily lives through chatbots such as Alexa, Siri, Google etc. We can ask questions about weather or music, shop for flowers or control various home electronics devices in a conversational manner. We believe that conversational interaction will dominate the next generation of interactions even in the IT Service Management world. To that effect, in this chapter we describe an AI infused conversational self-service system that enables a user to get precise answers to various domain specific questions in a natural conversational manner. These questions span the gamut of 5 W + H (What, Where, Which, Who, Why, How) queries in an increasingly refined conversational context including some that may require performing transactions on behalf of the user – such as adding memory to a virtual machine or starting/stopping a database.

In order for all chatbots to work effectively, two fundamental challenges need to be addressed: knowledge of the domain(s) for which questions need to be answered and linguistic capabilities to analyze the user utterances. E.g. for a typical consumer chatbot, such as Alexa, to answer a question such as "Will it rain in San Fransisco tomorrow?", it needs to be able to recognize three concepts in different domains (that "rain" is weather related, "tomorrow" is a temporal concept, and "San Fransisco" is a geographical location), along with the desired intent behind the question ("information seeking"). Having extracted these important aspects of the question, the chatbot needs to have access to a relevant service (a Weather Forecast service) which can provide a weather forecast for the desired location and time frame. Of course, the expected response to this question is (in the best case) a "yes" or "no" or perhaps "a likelihood indicator" like "unlikely" to "definitely". In this case, the chatbot has to transcribe the response from the weather service (which could be in terms of probability % for rain etc.) into a consumable response to the user.



K. Kloeckner et al., *Transforming the IT Services Lifecycle with AI Technologies*, SpringerBriefs in Computer Science,
https://doi.org/10.1007/978-3-319-94048-9_5

Several conversational authoring frameworks and services, such as Watson Conversation Service, enable a user to author and deploy a chatbot and provide components for (a) specifying "intents" which can be effectively answered (along with training utterance data to learn the intent labels) and (b) some type of entity model which can be defined for a domain of interest. Some chatbots also provide built in entity models for well understood concepts such as temporal, and geographical, etc. to ameliorate the task of creating a new chatbot for a new domain.

However, these chatbot services face the challenge of scalability in terms of Subject Matter Expert (SME) involvement in the creation of an effective and efficient chatbot. These challenges are exacerbated within the IT service management domain because the domain knowledge model is not well populated despite availability of an appropriate ontological model suitable for the IT Service Management domain.

Also, linguistic capabilities of the current chatbot are fairly limited, and especially so in the context of granular analysis of utterance. E.g. "I have a disk drive and battery failure" really reports two issues, "disk drive failure" and "battery failure"; so a simple entity model which recognizes "disk drive" and "battery" and "failure" separately is inadequate. Similarly, an expression such as "I do not have warranty" implies negation of having a warranty, so a simple extraction of entity "warranty" is inadequate.

There are additional challenges on linguistic capabilities for making the conversation more consumable. Consider an account ACME for whom the following question is asked "How many tickets did ACME have in 2017?" Having received the answer 1500 from the bot, the user's next question could be "and in 2016? ". This follow-up query needs to be resolved within the context of the prior question. So it is substituted with a new *complete* question ("How many tickets did ACME have in 2016?") that can now be effectively answered.

Even with a well populated domain knowledge and linguistic capabilities, there is another significant challenge that needs to be addressed for effective guided troubleshooting. This challenge is concerned with the reasoning that is required to make iterative progress towards problem determination and resolution. For example, when a user reports a "battery does not charge" issue, the chatbot is expected to walk the user through the resolution procedure. This procedure is encoded in the domain knowledge and comprises multiple diagnostic questions to follow up with (such as "is your laptop connected to power outlet?" etc.).

With these challenges and our overall goal in mind, we have identified the following process (in Fig. 1) for developing chatbot services for the IT Service Management domain. This approach provides a significant differentiation in the overall chatbot development process. The 7-day chatbot creation scenario (depicted in Fig. 1 column 4) is not meant to be a literal "no human touch" 1 week effort – but alludes to significant developer productivity that can be achieved by our novel development process.

We further refine the troubleshooting questions into those that can be handled through guided conversational troubleshooting with the self-service agent prompting a user with increasingly clarifying questions. This process leads to two possible

| Question Class | Type of answer | Microservice | Chatbot Creation Day* | Why do we believe we can do this? |
|---|---|---|---|---|
| Advise/Troubleshooting | Public Knowledge | Public Content | Day 1 | Shown through VA experiments – no special knowledge ingestion/curation needed |
| | Frequently Given Answers | Q and A Generator from FAQ docs | Day 2 | Automated generation of chat flows for platform level offering FAQ |
| | Guided Troubleshooting | • Question Analysis<br>• Content Analysis<br>• Knowledge Graph Creation & Reasoning | Day 3-4 | IBM Support: Product onboarding 6 months -> few days.<br>*IBM Support: Product chatbot Onboarding weeks -> days* |
| | Enterprise Knowledge Source | Orchestration over enterprise Knowledge Services | Day 5 | Demonstrated with Technical Health Check, Solution Assist, Global Clearing House, and W3 Community search service integrations |
| Browse (NLI to Structured Data) | Structured Data (summary, details etc) | NLI2Structured Data | Day 6 | *NLI to CogSolKB ~100 Person Hours (To Date)* |
| Act (NLI to Set of Services) | Take action on behalf of the user | NLI to a Set of Services (including chat flow generation to elicit required params) | Day 7 | *Work In Progress in IBM Support for SPSS License Key Renewal, Kenexa Password Reset etc., ICD/Service Now Catalog* |

**Fig. 1** Scalable chatbot development process

outcomes: the problem can be uniquely determined, or no unique problem can be determined. For the latter case, the conversational agent can pass the user to a human agent or let them create a support ticket. In some cases, the question can be answered based on Frequently Answered Questions (FAQ) which are documented in an organized manner. In such cases, the conversational agent can directly map the question to one of FAQs and provide the corresponding answer.

However, in the absence of such pre-existing knowledge, our experience suggests that a search engine that covers a broad spectrum of support vendor's sites, such as IBM, Microsoft, Oracle etc., and commonly used public forums, such as Stack Overflow, can provide reasonably good answers to a variety of questions. Since integrating such a search engine is usually an easy task, the chatbot can be instantiated relatively quickly using a search engine service alone. We will provide the results of empirical evaluations of this hypothesis later in this chapter.

Another key aspect of the conversational agent is its reliance on existing knowledge services in an enterprise. Most organizations have an internal search engine or a knowledge management system which externalizes that knowledge through services. Our conversational agent relies on such services operating in concert to provide an answer obtained from various sources. Using this approach avoids the challenge of re-ingesting the existing knowledge in yet another search engine.

However, as we mentioned earlier, the search engines can only provide coarse-grained answers to general questions. In order to provide a more effective and finer grain conversational interaction, and to answer various types of questions (for example about structured data), or perform actions, we need a suitable ontology to recognize key concepts and relationships in the IT Service Management Domain. Standards such as Common Information Model (CIM) [1] provide a strong foundation for this purpose. We leverage the Common Data Model (CDM), an IBM extension of CIM [2]. Figure 3 depicts the Common Data Model, which is a composition of models for various sub-domains.

Unfortunately, the Common Data Model focuses more on the Configuration Item aspect of IT Service Management and does not provide representation for support specific concepts such as symptoms or issues exhibited by various components, or

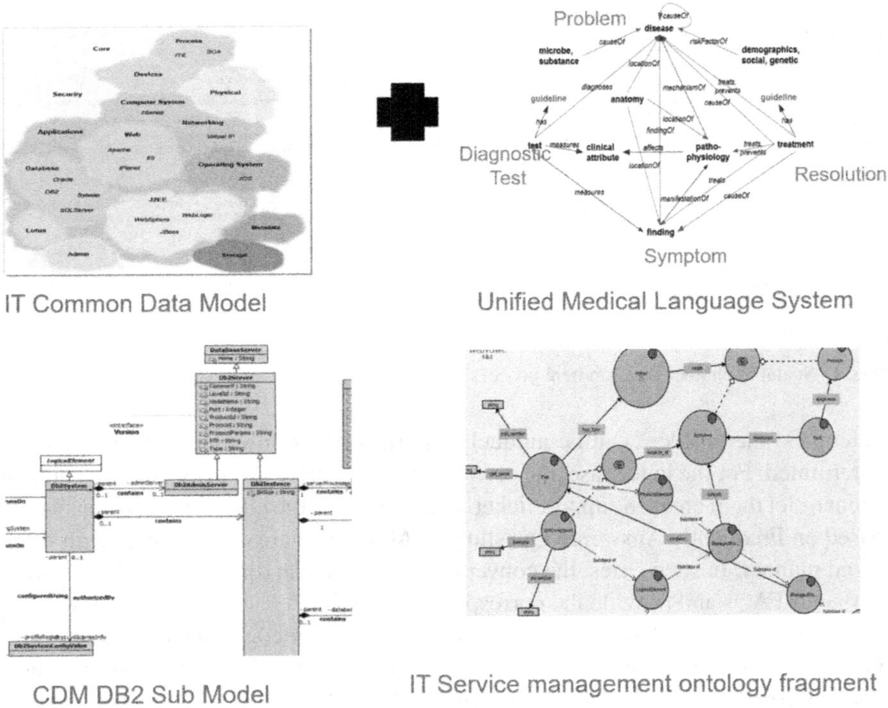


**Fig. 2** IT common data model, an example CDM sub model, unified medical language system, & a fragment of IT service management ontology

diagnostic procedures for identifying a particular problem, or ultimately, the resolution procedures for fixing the issues.

Fortunately, the health care domain has strong ontological foundations for these aspects in Unified Medical Language System (UMLS) [3]. We have borrowed these concepts from UMLS and extended the CDM with appropriate representation of support domain knowledge. Figure 2 depicts fragments of the IT Common Data Model and the UMLS and the adaptation for the IT Service management domain along with a fragment of unified IT Service Management Ontology.

However, a suitable ontology alone is not sufficient for an effective conversational self-service agent. As mentioned earlier, the ontology needs to be accompanied by strong linguistic analysis foundations. Ability to handle negation, co-reference, elliptical resolutions, etc. in input utterances is required for providing a consumable conversational experience. We leverage the strong foundations provided by the linguistic capabilities used in Watson Health, which in turn are extensions to the original Watson Jeopardy! NLP pipeline. Watson Health NLP engine is already aware of UMLS concepts and several capabilities available there could be applied to IT Service Management domain. The Watson Health pipeline provides out-of-the-box support for various NLP tasks such as:

- Deep Parsing and Predicate Representation of text
- Ontology Driven Parsing (Domain Specific Lexicons)

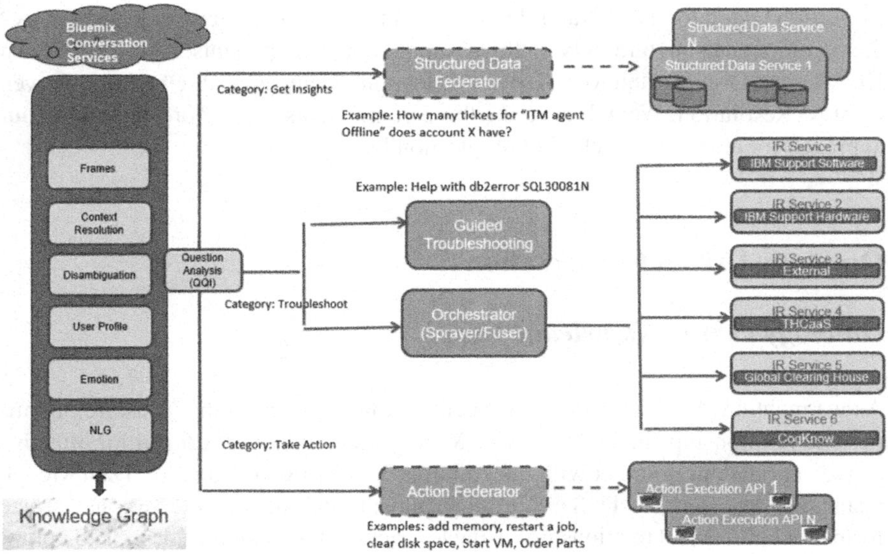


**Fig. 3** Architecture for conversational IT service management agent

- An extensible Pattern matching framework
- Negation Annotators
- Expanding over logically connected phrases
- Co-reference Resolution

The development of conversational self service agent builds on the capabilities described above, as depicted in Fig. 3. In addition to the Ontology Derived Knowledge Graph and the deeper linguistic components, Ontology Driven Question Analysis is another key component in the architecture. This component analyses an incoming utterance and classifies it in one of three supported intents: Structured Data question, Troubleshooting question or Take Action oriented question. The knowledge graph constructed from various knowledge sources guides this classification process. Depending on the intent, the utterance is delegated to an appropriate service to handle it. We will describe each of these services in detail in subsequent sections.

## Architecture

The development of the conversational self-service agent builds on the capabilities described above, as depicted in Fig. 3. The four main components that participate in the creation of conversational capability in the IT Service Management space are: (1) Guided Troubleshooting (2) Long Tail Search through Orchestrator (3) Structured Data Federator using Natural Language Interface to structured data and

(4) Action Federator using Natural Language Interface to Service Requests. Each of these components, in turn, rely on three foundational components: Ontology Driven Knowledge Graph, Ontology Driven Question Analysis and Ontology Driven Context Resolution. We will describe these components first before describing our approach for answering each kind of question later.

## Ontology Driven Conversation

### *Ontology Driven Knowledge Graph*

As we mentioned earlier, a domain specific knowledge graph that is aware of entities and relationships in the IT Service Management domain is critical for effective conversational engagement with the end user. We start with Common Data Model, a standard ontology for IT Service Management, and identify the various surface forms for entities and relationships using a variety of techniques as described below.

Entity extraction using distance supervision over an IT Support technical documentation corpus along with a variety of on-line resources (such as Wikipedia, DBPedia, Yago and etc.) employed for identification of alternate surface forms of various concepts used in the CDM. In future, we will explore deep learning based approaches to complement the distant supervision approaches.

We are interested in certain specific relationships between entities such as Hypernyms (is-a), Part-Whole, Cause-Effect, Property of, and other relationships which are mentioned explicitly in the CDM model. For identifying alternate surface forms of the relationships between entities we use a variety of techniques depending on the nature of the desired relationships as enumerated below:

- Rule-based (e.g. Hearst Patterns for Hypernyms [4])
- Distant supervision/learning using a variety of knowledge sources below
  - Wikipedia, web, glossaries etc. [5]
- Statistical (leveraging Word Embeddings) [6]
  - These techniques need a user to provide both Positive and Negative Examples for training
- Deep Learning based [7]
  - With dependency path between entities as a feature

Figure 4 shows a fragment of a knowledge graph constructed using our technique for troubleshooting a knowledge articles for IBM Storwize product, which describes the error code 673 along with corresponding diagnostic and resolution procedures. The Knowledge Graph shows the main symptom error code 673 which is connected to three problem nodes (along with a default No Problem node) along with the Diagnostic nodes for performing LED and other diagnostic tests.

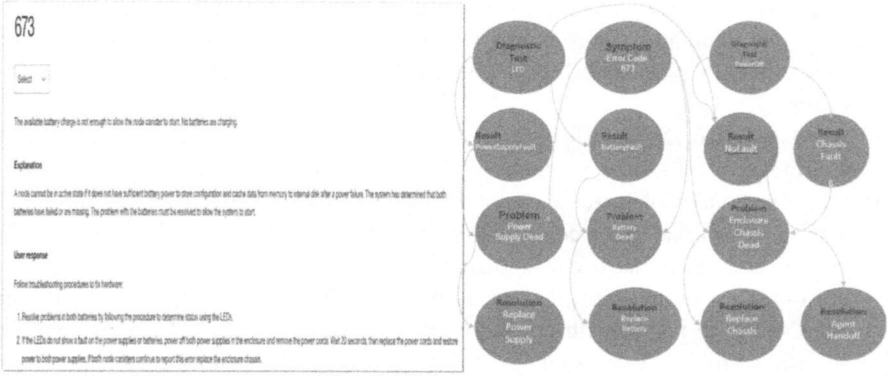


**Fig. 4** Example knowledge graph derived from a support article

## *Ontology Driven Question Analysis*

In addition to the Ontology Derived Knowledge Graph and the deeper linguistic components involved in it, Ontology Driven Question Analysis is another key component in the architecture. This component analyses an incoming utterance and classifies it in one of three supported intents: Structured Data question, Troubleshooting question or Take Action oriented question. The knowledge graph constructed from various knowledge sources guides this classification process. Depending on the intent, the utterance is delegated to an appropriate service to handle it. We will describe each of these services in detail in subsequent sections.

We treat the issue of question analysis as an information extraction problem rather than classification problem. Given a user utterance can mention various concepts of interest for the IT Service Management space, we consider the most important one to be the intent behind the question. Here we take a different approach to the problem intent classification: instead of proliferating several intents that a chat bot developer is expected to provide, we classify the intents into two broad categories which get further refined into three as mentioned earlier. These are “Tell me something” with the intent of seeking information or seeking problem determination help, and “Do something for me” which seeks execution of some action. Further, for a problem determination scenario in IT Service Management, the incoming utterance may mention a symptom that the user is experiencing or the activities they were performing when they experienced the symptoms. It may also include steps they have already tried to address the symptom on their own. With that view, we have built a question analysis pipeline which is guided by the ontology we have constructed. It allows to recognize various products/components mentioned in various text spans. The service uses the following annotators to accomplish the task:

- Subtree-based pattern matching where developers write templates and dictionaries associated to certain nodes which is used to generate a catalog of subtree patterns.

- Annotation Splitting where we canonicalize annotations which contain "and".
- Negation Annotator where words which have been negated using "not", "no", "never", "nor", "neither" etc. are used to show absence of a particular symptom.
- Wordnet-based Dictionaries are used to add Wordnet synsets directly to reduce the rote work of adding synonymous dictionary words.
- Smart Sentence Tokenizer is used to handle badly punctuated queries.
- Abbreviations and other colloquial short hand expressions (such as ASAP, pls etc) are converted into usual English.
- For ontology enabled parsing, we augment the lexicon used by the underlying deep semantic parser with ontology specific noun phrases and certain domain specific terms which are used as verbs: e.g. multi-word nouns such as "**lan to lan router**' or custom verbs such as '**ssh** into my machine', and custom adjectives or other parts of speech

## *Ontology Driven Context Resolution*

As mentioned earlier, a user may provide only a non-sentential utterance (such as "in 2016?" as one of the inputs. A chatbot needs to be able to resolve such a partial utterance and provide a relevant answer depending on the context of such interactions. We use ontological concepts in general and our unified ontology model in particular to resolve such partial inputs. In this section, we illustrate our approach.

Resolving context, like in the example above, manifests itself in several variants. In some cases, only the prior question is used to resolve the context. E.g. in the example above, if the prior user question was "how many tickets for Acme in 2017?", then a follow-on question "in 2016?" most likely refers to the same question but for year *2016*. In some other cases the previous answer is enough. E.g. consider the following interaction:

User: Show me the list of servers that I manage.
Bot: Answer is:

1. Abc.us.ibm.com
2. Def.us.ibm.com
3. Ghi.us.ibm.com

User: What is the CPU Utilization on the second one?

In this interaction, the second question refers to the server def.us.ibm.com

In other interactions, context resolution requires both the previous question as well as the previous answer.

Here we present our approach only for the cases where the previous question is sufficient for resolving the context.

The key intuition behind our approach involves type substitution – both at entity and relationship levels. In the example above, given that "2016" is a temporal concept (and so is 2017), the most likely substitution which will lead to a type consistent sentence completion is replacing 2017 with 2016 and reformulating the original sentence.

As another example, if the user's initial question is "How much memory does foo have", we infer that *foo* is the name of an instance of **server** type. (based on the contextual information in the configuration database as described below). If the next question says "and bar?", again our linguistic analysis detects that *bar* is the name of another instance of **server** type (again based on the contextual configuration data) and substitutes "foo" with "bar" and reconstitutes the complete question for subsequent analysis.

Both these were examples of compatible "instance" level substitutions – where the entities that were being replaced were instances of a given type.

In other cases, the substitution could involve the entity type itself. For example, consider the question: "What languages are supported by Offering A?". Here, in our ontological system, an "Offering" is a type (with A as its instance), and "language" is another type with "support" as the relationship between offering and language. Further, in our ontology, SLA is another type which also has "support" relationship with an offering.

If the user asks a follow up question "and SLAs?", our ontology driven linguistic analysis infers that the most likely substitution which will preserve the semantic relationships mentioned in the original question would be to replace "language" with "SLA".

As an example of relationship substitution, consider that the ontology also has another type called "system" that is related with Offering through a relationship labeled "manages". If now, the user asks the follow-on question "and systems managed?", our ontology driven linguistic analysis infers that the most semantic preserving substitution in this case is to replace "language" with "system" and "support" with "manage".

## Troubleshooting Questions

As shown in the architecture diagram in Fig. 3, our current chatbot supports two strategies for answering questions which are classified to be troubleshooting oriented: Guided Troubleshooting and Long Tail Search through Orchestrator. In this section we describe each strategy.

### *Guided Troubleshooting*

Guided Troubleshooting is a step-by-step way in which an expert troubleshoots a user query. Troubleshooting follows a pattern of question-answering where in response to a user query e.g. "I am having trouble booting my server", several disambiguating questions can be asked, e.g. did you mean a linux or windows servers. Sometimes diagnostic tests are performed by the agent to test some conditions e.g. "Can you run this command on the server?". Based on the results of the diagnostic steps a specific action could be recommended.

Automatically doing guided troubleshooting in a conversation setting is a research challenge.

In this section, we describe our approach to handling troubleshooting questions which require a guided interaction between a human user and the chatbot. We will use the knowledge graph derived in Fig. 4 to illustrate. The first panel of Fig. 5, assumes that the user reports the following issue "v7k is failed due to batteries. error code 673" as the initial utterance. When the chatbot finds an appropriate node in the Knowledge Graph for symptom 673, it realizes that there are four possible alternative problems as shown in the first panel.

At this point, the chatbot reasons that by performing the LED diagnostic test, the user can help prune the hypothetical problem space in half. So, the chatbot can formulate a question back to the user asking them about the status shown on the LED as shown in the second panel in Fig. 5.

If the user responds to the LED question with a BatteryFault result, then it could be determined that the battery is dead, and it needs to be replaced. This is illustrated in the third panel in Fig. 5.

## *Long Tail Search Through Orchestrator*

In some situations, the answer to the user's initial question may not be found through the knowledge graph-based strategy. In this case the best alternative may be to search for a relevant answer in available knowledge sources. Here we take a novel approach of integrating a variety of knowledge services, one or more of which may have content that is relevant for the question. This approach is in contrast to that of ingesting various knowledge sources as a single collection in an Information

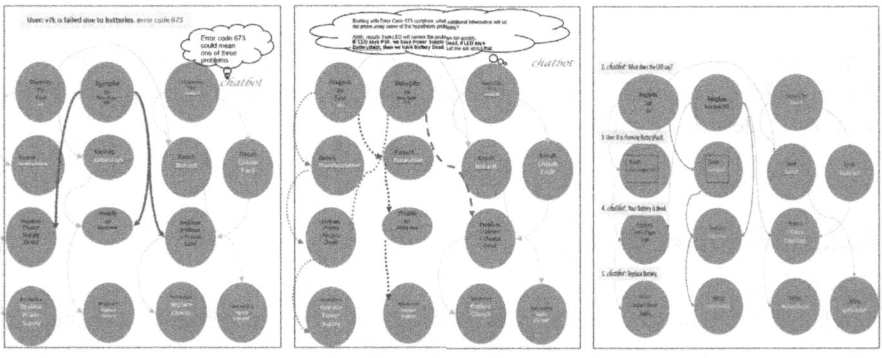


**Fig. 5** Illustrative chatbot reasoning process and conversation flow

Retrieval engine (such as Apache Solr or Elastic Search). In this approach, we may not be able to provide a precise or a guided response to the user, but we may be able to provide a coarse grained response (in the form of a web page) that may still prove to be useful.

We chose this orchestrated (or federated) search approach because in a typical large enterprise information resides in distributed data sources (and some of these data sources have knowledge services which expose that data). For instance, within IBM, there are knowledge services that provide access to technical support data for various IBM products, another knowledge service that allows searching over various internal Wiki pages, yet another knowledge service that allows searching over historical customer engagement data etc. It is not practical to move all this content to one repository which can then be searched. Moreover, as the example knowledge services mentioned earlier indicate, such data sources are quite heterogeneous in nature and treating them as one collection will be technically challenging.

Our approach also leverages the "wisdom of the crowd" approach in small by integrating multiple knowledge services. If a given document is returned as a relevant response by multiple knowledge services for a given question, then we can be certain that the answer is indeed valuable and we can be even more confident in its relevance.

Our orchestrator component, therefore, plays a significant role in improving the effectiveness of long tail searches – on one hand it makes the task of integrating a new knowledge service easy and on the other hand, through the power of "wisdom of the crowd", it provides more relevant suggestions for an input question.

Each troubleshooting question which cannot be handled through the guided troubleshooting process leveraging the knowledge graph is relayed to the orchestrator component. The orchestrator, in turn, sprays the question to each of the knowledge services that is registered with it. The orchestrator performs a merge of the results returned by each knowledge service based on the associated confidence scores. It also performs another text similarity check between the query and the suggestions returned by each service before collating the results and boosting the scores of suggestions which are returned by multiple knowledge services.

Some knowledge services may not return a confidence score corresponding to each suggestion, in which case we use rank reciprocal as the proxy for confidence score (essentially the confidence score for a suggestion is the numeric reciprocal of its ranking in the list – thus suggestion in first place has confidence score of 1, that in second is 1/2 etc.). This is a standard practice in the Information Retrieval community.

## Natural Language Interface to Structured Data

Structured data is an important source of information in IT Service management. As we show in the architecture diagram in Fig. 3, a user can ask a question about such structured data in natural language. In this section we describe our approach to an

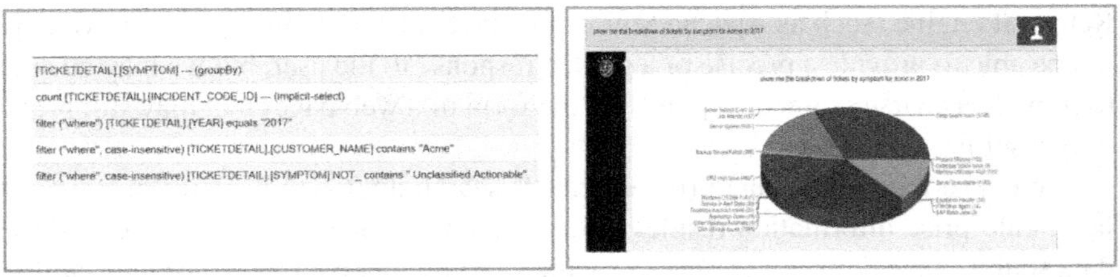


**Fig. 6** Intermediate query and the Visual rendering for "Show me the breakdown of tickets by symptom for ACME in 2017"

ontology driven natural language interface to structured data. Given that the structured data in our scope is also from the IT Service Management domain (Configuration Items, Incident and Change Tickets etc.), we are able to map it to the Information Technology Infrastructure Library (ITIL) section of the Common Data Model. We have extended the ITIL model with additional attributes from the UMLS concepts described above. For example, an incident ticket is associated with a symptom which is reported as part of the incident, and each incident also has a resolution that was performed to close it. ITIL also provides a natural mapping to other relevant metadata such as accounts for which the incidents are reported etc.

We provide a mapping between our ontology and the concrete database schema where the data resides. This allows us to interpret the questions posed in conceptual terms that are familiar to the user and to translate them into relevant database SQL queries.

For a natural language question such as "Show me the breakdown of tickets by symptom for ACME in 2017", we use ontology driven linguistic analysis to identify that "tickets" is a concept which is mentioned in the ITIL component sub model in CDM. Further, we recognize that "symptom" represents a concept related to the ticket entity based on our unified ontology, and we recognize that "ACME" is the name of an *instance* of an ontological concept Account, also referred to as Customer, (which is provided as an instance dictionary). Finally, we recognize that 2017 is a temporal concept; and that the term "breakdown" indicates a quantity summarization intent.

Results of this processing coupled with mapping to the concrete database schema leads to an intermediate query as shown in the first panel in Fig. 6. As we can see, the intermediate summary (in this case 'groupBy') query contains appropriate filters on various columns of the ticket table.

Running such a query results in a visual rendering of the data shown in the second panel in Fig. 6.

## Natural Language Interface to Service Requests

We also provide a conversational model of interaction for executing Service Requests automatically (e.g. "start service sshd on server foo"). Since each of these service requests is also in the domain of IT Service Management, it has a

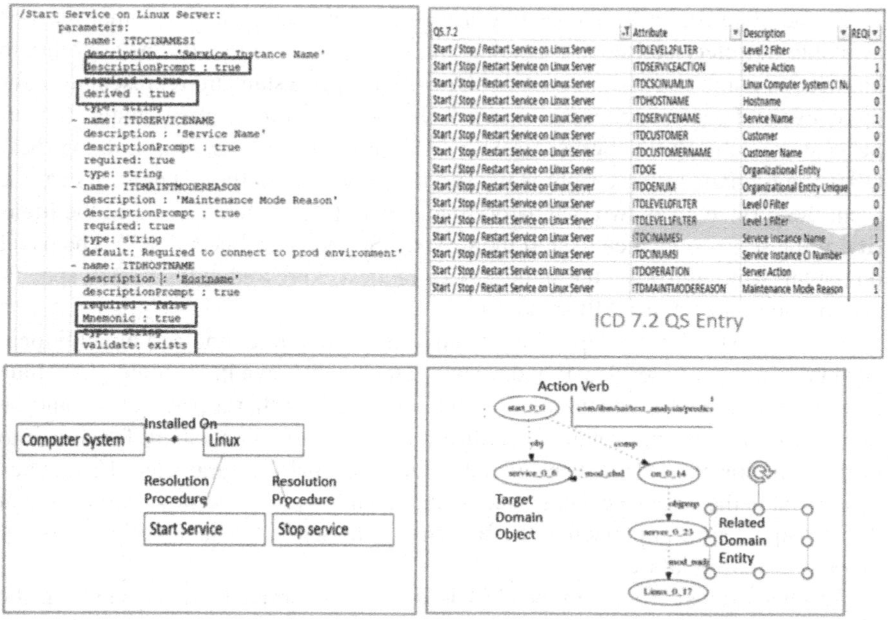


**Fig. 7** Specification of an example Catalog Service

corresponding association with the unified CDM + UMLS ontology we have presented earlier. We view each Service Request as a potential **Resolution Procedure** for some component in the Common Data Model. E.g. a service request "Start Database Db2 on Linux Server" is associated as a Resolution procedure with the DB2 Database component in the CDM. This approach serves a two-fold purpose. First, when a user explicitly issues a Service Request (such as "Start DB2 database XYZ on Server Foo"), we can quickly check if a Service Request with a matching signature exists in the constructed knowledge graph. A second, but equally important purpose is that we now have a potential resolution procedure if a user reports a symptom where (s)he cannot connect to a DB2 database. Our guided troubleshooting procedure described in an earlier section may detect (after a few debugging conversational turns with the user) that the database the user is trying to connect to is not started. In which case, our chatbot can offer to take that action on behalf of the user, as long as appropriate access control credentials are presented.

This conceptual relationship for an example service request ("Start Service on Linux Server") is depicted on panels at the bottom of Fig. 7 that illustrate how the Service Request is associated with appropriate ontological concepts in our domain knowledge graph. On the left is the association of "Start Service" as a resolution procedure for the Linux operating system which is installed on a computer system. The panel on the right shows the representation in which this information is stored. Note that we identify an "action verb" such as "start" to reflect that a state changing operation is implied and that the target object of this action verb is "service" and that the mentioned service is on a Linux Server.

To facilitate the task of ingesting a given set of service requests that may be available in a Service Request Catalog and to associate them with the appropriate knowledge graph components, we use OpenAPI [8] as a standard representation for the catalog of service requests. Figure 7 shows an example service request (Start Service on Linux Virtual Server) from IBM Control Desk Quick Start Catalog (ICD QS). The top Panel on the right is the service as defined in the ICD QS. As can be seen, the service takes two mandatory parameters (the service name and the **identity** of the server on which to start the service "Service Instance Name"). The panel on the left hand illustrates the same service request expressed in the YAML specification notation for OpenAPI standard.

We have extended the OpenAPI standard to be able to define certain additional attributes for a given service. E.g. one such extension (shown in the highlighted blue box around the word "mnemonic" on the left panel) is that a parameter could be optional in the original catalog specification but is more convenient for a user to provide. In this example, the specification indicates that the parameter "Hostname" is optional in the original catalog specification, but is a preferred way for the chatbot user to supply (in comparison to the **Identity** of the server – a mandatory parameter in the original signature).

Another extension to the OpenAPI is through a "derived" value flag; e.g. the "Service Instance Name" which is a mandatory parameter, but as mentioned above, is not a convenient information for a user to remember is a derived attribute. Its value is derived the "hostname" optional parameter.

Another important extension is the use of "validate" flag as associated with "hostname" parameter in the left panel. This flag indicates that the supplied parameter value needs to be validated against some known context for it to be valid. In the IT Service Management Service Request domain, we also use knowledge of instance level configuration items from the Configuration Management database (CMDB) as our context. A CMDB essentially provides an instance level view that corresponds to the IT Common Data Model that we already use and thus provides a very powerful mechanism to leverage our ontology in yet another dimension.

This validity check enables us to better identify the target of the service request based on the user utterance. E.g. in the utterance "start process sshd on server foo", knowing that "foo" is a server, in our CMDB, and it is a Linux server, will allow to infer that the desired service is Start Process sshd on Linux Server foo. On the other hand, based on a knowledge that foo is an AIX server, inference would provide a different target API (Start Process sshd on AIX server).

Use of instance level views in the CMDB coupled with ontology driven linguistic processing allows us to infer the most relevant intended target Service Request. Figure 8 illustrates various input user utterances that our chatbot can handle. The top row in the left hand panel illustrates a case where the user just requests "Start Service on Linux Server" without providing the server or the service name.

Our linguistic analysis (as shown in the dependency parse tree of the utterance in the third column of first row in the left panel) identifies that there is an action verb "start" in the request and the target object for that request is a "Service" on a "Linux Server". We use this dependency tree to match with the corresponding entries in our

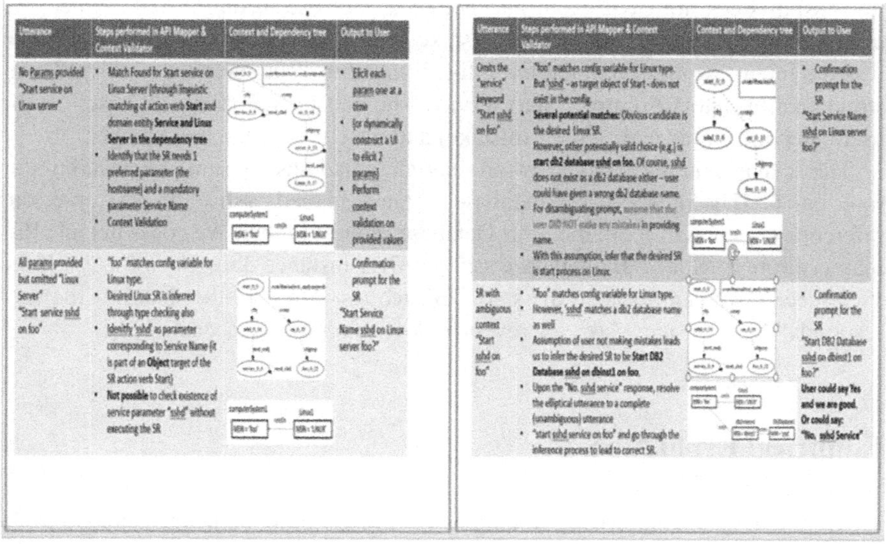

**Fig. 8** Potential variants of an Service Request Utterance

knowledge graph that corresponds to "Linux Server" component in the graph. We find that a service request that matches the action verb (*start*) and the target object (*service*) is available. We further find that this service expects values of two parameters (*hostname* and *service name*) from the user. We thus prompt the user to supply these two values. Assuming that the user says "foo" for hostname, and "sshd" for service name, we first validate that "foo" is a valid server name in the CMDB. Unfortunately, we cannot validate that "sshd" is a valid service name. But at this point, we confirm from the user that they would like to "Start Service *sshd* on Linux Server *foo*. If the user accepts, then we construct a payload with the appropriate parameter values and the service name for a back end execution engine to execute.

The bottom row in the left panel illustrates another scenario, where the user just says "Start service sshd on foo". Here the user has omitted the "Linux Server" phrase from the request. But, our ontology driven linguistic analysis detects first that "foo" is the name of a CMDB instance of type "Linux Server". Coupled with this "type information", we again perform a match against the knowledge graph for component "Linux Server" and find a match with "Start Service". Since we have all the parameters that we need, we provide an affirmative prompt to the user ("Start service sshd on Linux Server foo?") and if the user accepts, we replicate the payload construction and execution process.

The right panel of Fig. 8 illustrates even more interesting variants. In the top row, the user just says "Start sshd on foo". Again, using the type of *foo* (Linux Server) as inferred from ontology driven linguistic analysis as an anchor point, we find that there are several candidate services that have action verb "start" – such as the implied target "start *service*" as well as "start *database*". Here, we leverage the fact that "sshd" does not exist as an instance of a database in our CMDB. Since, we assume that the user did not make a mistake in specifying the database name if that was the intent, we infer that the more likely match is "start service sshd" and construct an affirmatory prompt ("Start service sshd on Linux Server foo?"), so that the user can confirm (or realize their mistake) and we can proceed accordingly.

The scenario on the bottom row on the right panel has the same request, but this time our CMDB indeed has a database instance named "sshd". In this case, our inference engine will score the Start Database request higher. We construct an affirmatory prompt "Start DB2 database sshd on DB2 instance dbinst1 on foo?"). If the user accepts we can dispatch the start DB2 request. On the other hand, if the user responds "No. Service sshd", we revert back to the previous scenario.

## Empirical Evaluation

We have conducted empirical evaluations of several components presented here. In this section, we summarize the findings.

### *Ontology Driven Question Analysis*

In addition to our chatbot, this capability is also deployed to elicit better descriptions from the user at the time of support case creation. The intuition behind eliciting better descriptions is that it will help a support engineer resolve the case faster. Symptoms, already performed diagnosis/resolution attempts (if any), and intent (whether troubleshooting or taking specific action) are essential attributes of a case. Before we enable this capability on a particular support product, we performed the ontology driven question analysis of a sample of historical cases and had the resulting annotations evaluated by support engineers who are experts in those products. The support engineers marked each generated annotation as either correct or incorrect (and if incorrect provided a correct version). Using this evaluation, we measured precision and recall metrics (along with the standard F measure). In the early days, when the capability was still being developed, the results for initial set of four products had 80% precision, 72% Recall and 76% F value.

Subsequent versions of the capability were applied to a next set of 11 products that resulted in 73% precision, 73% Recall and 73% F value. Using this experience, we evolved the capability even further. Similar support engineer evaluation of the latest set of four products which are onboarded on the capability show 92% Precision, 94% Recall and 93% F value.

These results gave us enough confidence to onboard the remaining products (several hundred in number) without going through an up-front support engineer evaluation for each of those products. We still perform a random evaluation of annotations produced on cases, but the capability has significantly helped us with the scalability aspects (and enables our envisioned 7-day chatbot creation scenario depicted in Fig. 1.)

## *Troubleshooting Questions*

We conducted several experiments to evaluate the troubleshooting questions capabilities of the conversational chatbot. In the first experiment, we asked 21 service architects who are technical experts in various domains (such as Networking, Storage, Database, Windows and Linux Servers etc) to ask the chatbot ten questions of their choice. Each of these questions was meant to have troubleshooting intent (thereby following the orchestrator path – at the time we did not have the guided troubleshooting capability in the chatbot). Each architect also evaluated the top three chatbot responses on a scale of Resolved, Contributed, and Not Relevant (Resolved means one of the three answers was exactly what they were looking for, Contributed means one of the answers were extremely helpful but not perfect, and Not Relevant means none of the top three answers was relevant to the question). We considered either a Resolved or a Contributed rating to mean the question had a good answer.

We had a total of 202 questions for which 662 responses were provided. 141 out of the 202 questions had a good answer (giving the chatbot an overall accuracy of 70%). Further, 85 out of these 141 answers (42% overall) were rated as Resolved. This experiment was conducted early in the chatbot development process and we identified two major areas of improvement as well. One major area concerned with misclassified intents. Out of the 61 questions that did not have good rating, 37 had a misclassified intent (in that the Question Analysis classifier labeled the question as something other than troubleshooting – and hence the question did not reach the orchestrator). The remaining 24 questions which had answers rated "Not Relevant" pointed to content gaps in the knowledge services that were registered with the orchestrator.

As shown in the architecture diagram of Fig. 3, our orchestrator has several knowledge services registered – some knowledge services have internal IBM Knowledge sources, other knowledge services have externally visible IBM knowledge services and we also have integrated an external public content search engine. We wanted to evaluate the contribution of various knowledge services and their sources.

Figure 9 provides a further breakdown of the results. One highlight to note is the value of publicly available content in providing correct answers. More than 85% of the good answers came from either IBM Externally available knowledge or publicly available content. For some IBM specific topics (such as those involving Migration or Transition/Transformation of new clients into an IBM environment), we identified content gaps that needs to be bridged.

In another experiment, we took questions used in training data (a set of Question-Answer pairs defined for Microsoft Outlook domain) used to train another chatbot. We used 148 unique questions identified from this training set as input to our chatbot. We had to prefix the questions with a product identifying phrase ("Microsoft Outlook 2013" to make the context explicit for the orchestrator queries). We evaluated the answers received from the chatbot in a similar manner (we could not use the

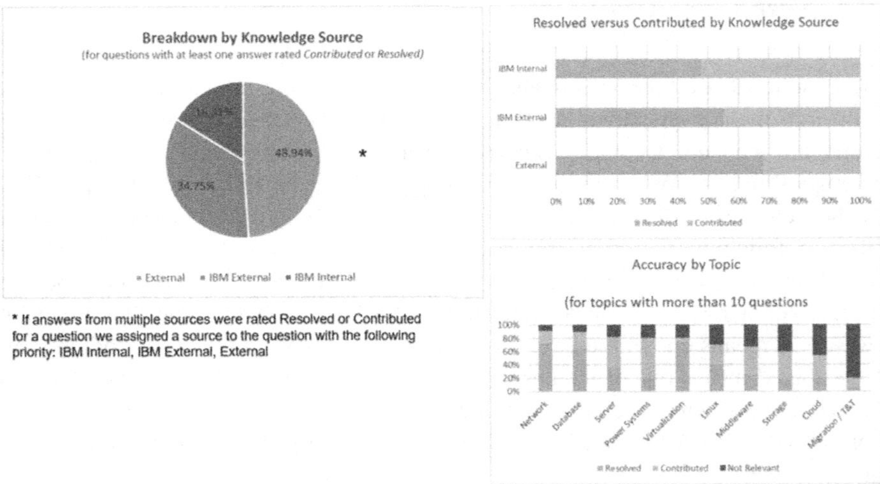


**Fig. 9** Importance pubic available content

answers from the original training set since they were from curated documents as opposed to web URLs that our orchestrator suggested).

In this experiment, 120 out of 148 question had a good answer resulting in an accuracy rating of 81%. Furthermore, 112 questions (76% overall) had an answer with Resolved rating. As in the previous experiment, a significant fraction of the good answers came from public searchable content (primarily from Microsoft support sites).

As mentioned earlier, the answers in the training data came from curated document sources. Most of these answers were step by step answers to the associated question (in some cases the answers also contained instructional videos). While such content is very useful for novice users (who are not tech savvy), there is a cost premium associated with it. Whereas the public searchable content may not be as novice-user friendly, is available for free. Such a tradeoff needs to be evaluated based on the target chatbot user profile. However, the value of public searchable content demonstrates the feasibility of creating a chatbot which can provide coarse grained answers (as URLs) to any user question and thus enables us to fulfill our day 0 goal outlined in the 7-day scenario in Fig. 1.

## Conclusion and Future Work

In this chapter, we have presented an approach to building a scalable, ontology driven conversational assistant for the IT Service Management domain. We leverage concepts and linguistic capabilities developed for the health care domain and re-purpose it for our target domain. Our conversational assistant can answer two broad categories of questions ("Tell me something" and "Do something for me") where the responses to the "Tell me something" could require interacting with a structured data source (such as a relational database). Another novel aspect of answering the "tell me something" question involves guided troubleshooting based on a knowledge graph constructed from the underlying knowledge sources. We have also presented empirical results which demonstrate the effectiveness and scalability of our approach.

In future, we will continue to refine the linguistic capabilities to improve the overall accuracy of the conversational assistant. In certain cases, the knowledge articles contain either software product commands or log trace to illustrate the relevant symptoms. Linguistic analysis in the presence of such mixed language styles provides another set of challenges to address. Another area of enhancement is concerned with improving the reasoning process used in the guided troubleshooting process. We are also working on augmenting the ontological concepts and relationships to areas of IT Service Management not represented adequately in CDM, the foundational ontology we use. This includes identifying concepts for representing various applications and modern digital devices.

**Acknowledgements** This work represents efforts of several contributors. We would like to acknowledge the significant contributions from Gargi Dasgupta, Yu Deng, Ruchi Mahindru, Jin Xiao, Anup Kalia and Sethu Subramaniam.

## References

1. https://www.dmtf.org/standards/cim
2. https://www.ibm.com/developerworks/community/groups/service/html/communitystart?communityUuid=e1effee6-69a2-4c91-90aa-347f79d0030e
3. https://www.nlm.nih.gov/research/umls/
4. Hearst M (1992) Automatic acquisition of hyponyms from large text corpora. In: Proceedings of COLING-92. Nantes, France, pp 539–545
5. Snow R, Jurafsky D, Ng A (2005) Learning syntactic patterns for automatic hypernym discovery. In: Proceedings of NIPS 17, Bonn, Germany
6. Bollegala D, Maehara T, Kawarabayashi K (2015) Embedding semantic relations into word representations. In: Proceedings of IJCAI, Buenos Aires, Argentina, pp. 1222–1228
7. Huang L, Sil A, Ji H, Florian R (2017) Improving slot filling performance with attentive neural networks on dependency structures. In: Empirical Methods in Natural Language Processing (EMNLP), Copenhagen, Denmark
8. https://www.openapis.org/

# Practical Advice for Introducing AI into Service Management

In the following chapter, we summarize best practices for the introduction of AI in service management, for the benefit of IT leaders and their teams. In our view, the following points are essential:

1. Introducing AI has to be part of a **holistic strategy** of transforming service management. It requires both top-down leadership support as well as community engagement, and clear communication of expected results as well as limitations. It is not just about selection of technologies and training of practitioners but has deep implications for processes and organizational culture.
2. AI has great potential to significantly change and elevate the work performed by human experts by identifying automation opportunities. This requires different skills and organizational setups and should be used to accelerate **agile transformation**. We suggest to run the introduction of AI as an agile project, with disciplined iterations and clear measurements [1].
3. A successful AI strategy for IT requires establishing a **data-driven approach and culture**. Understanding IT operational data (especially ticket data for incidents and service requests) is a prerequisite to knowing what questions to ask and how to accelerate the training of AI.
4. When building ground truths, leverage your organizational knowledge and treat it as an enterprise asset, but also be prepared to challenge hidden assumptions. Establish an **end-to-end knowledge lifecycle strategy** that engages the subject matter experts.

We will discuss these points in a little more detail, drawing on the authors' experience across IBM's outsourced accounts. However, we strongly feel that the same approach can be applied by a CIO organization acting as an internal service provider.



K. Kloeckner et al., *Transforming the IT Services Lifecycle with AI Technologies*, SpringerBriefs in Computer Science,
https://doi.org/10.1007/978-3-319-94048-9_6

## Establishing a Holistic Strategy for AI Applying Agile Transformation Principles

While it is important to get rapid exposure to AI by establishing projects with hands-on experimentation, it is imperative to set direction and context early on.

- An AI strategy needs to be communicated from the top of the organization and linked to its transformation goals. It is important to remind all stakeholders that AI is not the technology flavor of the month, but a 'tool' to better leverage the data and the knowledge the organization already has. Thus, an AI strategy needs to be anchored in a data strategy and knowledge management strategy.
- Clearly articulate expected business outcomes. Set up formal stakeholder engagement with a lightweight governance structure. This needs to include business leadership.
- Ensure a critical mass of skills. Set up a center of competency, potentially virtual.
- Build a skills plan that enables the broad community (technical and non-technical) to get some exposure and to understand how it affects the skills they will require in the future. Consider hackathons and innovation competitions and other community events to foster a spirit of AI-based innovation.
- Encourage exploration of and participation in open source communities. GitHub is an excellent source of AI related code. The cloud offerings of major vendors are quickly becoming more powerful and are quite comparable.
- Build a multi-stage roadmap for introduction of AI, with clearly defined measurable goals for each stage. We have achieved great results with a 'lean startup' approach.
- Be prepared to take on both inflated expectations as well as fears related to AI. It is helpful to emphasize that while AI, combined with automation, may replace lower-skilled tasks, many AI applications require training by experts and primarily augment human intelligence.
- Eliminating repetitive tasks and providing support for better decision making and problem-solving changes the nature of work in IT (as in other areas). Make the introduction of AI into operational processes part of a broader process re-design that emphasizes agile practices and organization.

## Building a Data-Driven Culture

As demonstrated in this book, we have now reached a point in which we can use operational data to fuel an AI-led feedback loop steering automation and augmenting human decision making. Here are a few recommended principles:

1. **Create a data lake:** This holds your operational data, like problem tickets, service requests, configuration data, change records, root cause analysis, resource

consumption history, etc. It will provide the basis for discovering patterns through correlation of data from different sources that could not otherwise be detected. For instance, collecting historical data across hundreds of thousands of servers can allow you to predict (and preempt) server outages. Similarly, analyzing thousands of change records allows you to more accurately assess the risk of changes, which often is classified incorrectly by IT personnel.

2. **Establish comprehensive monitoring and event management, feeding into the data lake:** While implementing APIs for the data lake is foundational to growing content from different sources, the main conduit is the event management system. It is very important to reduce the proportion of events that turn into incidents that require attention. By fine tuning event correlation mechanisms, nearly 90% of events can be filtered out.
3. **Let problem tickets tell you what to automate and to identify root causes of problems:** Typically, a Pareto distribution applies, most tickets fall into a small number of categories, and thus automation becomes economically viable for about 80% of incidents. Additionally, applying machine learning technologies can automatically identify non-actionable tickets, and the use of text analysis can identify common root causes. Together, these technologies can enable full automatic resolution or auto-assist resolution of the majority of tickets flowing through the incident management automation system. For auto-resolved tickets, mean time to recovery can improve by up to 90%.
4. **Establish a continuous feedback loop:** Every action leaves a trace in the data lake, which should be routinely analyzed for improvement opportunities. It is important to make this an ongoing iterative process. For instance, as a service-provider you can continually assess the effectiveness of automation and compare across accounts to bring every client to best of breed.
5. **Make data and insights visible and create a data-driven culture:** Through dashboards and self-service analytics, you can make data the foundation of any conversation between stakeholders. These insights dashboards increasingly have a **business perspective**. For instance, you can group information pertaining to IT resources for the business service they support, so that IT issues are made visible in a business context. You can use dashboards to create transparency, and to drive a 'get to green' culture.
6. **Establish a data science competency:** In today's data-driven era, the data scientist has a distinct profession and career path that needs nurturing. Consider hiring a Chief Data Officer and establishing a center of competency and a community for data scientists.
7. **Take a holistic approach:** Adopting a data-driven continual improvement approach has a profound impact on organization, process and skills. You have to address all aspects to make a data-driven transformation sustainable.

All the insights gained through a data-driven continual improvement process will feed and enhance your knowledge bases. This links the data lifecycle to a knowledge lifecycle based on systematic curation of expert knowledge which you can leverage into assistant and advisor tools for all stages of the service delivery lifecycle. For example, you can use text analysis and concept extraction technologies to map client requirements to a client solution catalog, with the aim to speed up the process of solution co-creation between your clients and your solution managers.

## Establishing a Knowledge Lifecycle Strategy

The following observations and recommendations are based on the IT Services industry but can be applied in any industry.

Let us first review some key problems knowledge-based organizations are facing today.

- Knowledge is perishable and shifting, it needs to be updated continuously and consistently.
- The knowledge required for any given domain is growing exponentially, and spread across many different sources, inside and outside the organization. For instance, a storage architect today increasingly needs knowledge about software-defined infrastructure even beyond storage, both from vendor information and through community sources. For any individual expert, it is more and more difficult to stay on top of even just their own core domain.
- Experts are often deep only in a few subjects, leading to suboptimal answers for other, related areas. In IT, it is hard to find architects that can address complex solutions spanning multiple technical domains. Designing such solutions often requires assembling entire teams, which is exacerbated by time pressures and conflicting demands on the available skills.
- Top experts are often geographically dispersed, making it difficult to get a 'second opinion' or peer reviews in a timely fashion, even with the help of communication tools.
- Top experts are so much in demand that they rarely spend enough of their time on sharing knowledge and grooming the next level of experts, unless a very strong culture makes it part of their core duties.
- Knowledge is often applied inconsistently. Within large expert communities competing views or practices can emerge. Best practices may atrophy into tribal customs without being challenged and improved continually.
- Training is time-consuming and takes away resources from front-line work, and often is performed only on a best effort basis.
- In some areas, experts are retiring faster than new ones are coming up (e.g. mainframe), or experts are so rare that they are susceptible to poaching (e.g. Software Defined Networking), threatening the loss of organizational capability.

These challenges need to be addressed systematically, through process, tools and culture, and with explicit focus on the community of experts and its leaders. The following elements are essential for success:

- A systematic approach to capturing and maintaining organizational knowledge that becomes engrained in the culture and processes and addresses the entire life cycle of knowledge.
- A strong knowledge community with a technical leadership that acts as stewards of the knowledge life cycle
- Rewards, role models and executive commitment to foster a culture of knowledge sharing and social curation of knowledge
- Strong metrics that demonstrate the business value of investment in the knowledge life cycle

The cultural and organizational elements described above must be reinforced by introducing tools that build and maintain knowledge bases in a systematic fashion and make them available for practical use. These tools integrate the knowledge of the broad community inside and outside the organization, and they also provide assistance and advice to individual technical experts at every level. In fact, they become virtual 'buddies', allowing an individual to draw on the collective 'wisdom' of their peer group, and to reap the benefits of their own contributions to the collective pooling of knowledge.

Thus, these tools drive consistency in the application of knowledge while providing immediate payback for the investment in knowledge bases. A few areas from infrastructure technology services where knowledge-based tools have shown great impact are

- Recommending a solution design based on request for proposal documents, reference architectures and existing solution building blocks
- Performing technical health checks and recommending improvement actions
- Analyzing complex problems

In all these cases, large amounts of information need to be processed and organized. Recent advances of AI technology are making this possible, among them

- Text conversion (with retention of structure to facilitate understanding) to handle the many different types of documents like manuals, white papers, tech reports, reference architectures or best practice guidance that form the unstructured body of knowledge of today's experts
- Advanced concept extraction, semantic parsing, text understanding. For instance, when processing requirements documents, the functional requirement extraction employs syntactic and semantic parsing tags and language tokens to build abstract patterns of requirements using POS (part-of-speech) tags and typed dependencies
- Constraint programming techniques and constraint optimization methods to allow trade-offs among solutions
- Supervised learning with
  - Upfront training set in order to make the tool production ready
  - Constant refinement and augmentation of knowledge base through annotation mechanisms utilized by experts

- Conversational user interfaces based on Natural Language Processing to facilitate interactions and sharing
- Ontologies and data linkage/federation techniques across knowledge domains.

When building and testing these tools, it is important to make the technical community a key part of the process and to set the right expectations concerning the use and role of AI, and to deal with common objections up-front. For instance, we have found that inflated expectations concerning accuracy can slow acceptance. These expectations often mask fears that AI-based tools can and will completely supplant experts, rather than enable them to perform better. For instance, 100% accuracy for a recommendation tool is not necessary for it to be useful to assist experts, especially given that the performance of human experts usually falls far short of that benchmark.

We now have enough initial experience to be very optimistic about sustained benefits, such as more consistent application of knowledge with higher quality results, the ability to direct sparse expert resources to the most complex problems and speedier response and deeper levels of interactions between stake holders. For instance, AI-based automatic processing of response documents is showing promise to lead to faster client co-creation of IT solutions. We also expect that the increased empowerment of technical leaders as stewards of the knowledge life cycle will lead to better training, attraction and retention of senior experts.

## Conclusion

While it is still early days for AI in IT services management, it's important for every IT organization to develop a strategy for leveraging AI for improved delivery quality. Organizations that have gone through transformation will quickly discover that the best practices learned there apply to an AI initiative as well. On the other side, a systematic approach with stakeholder engagement and a disciplined agile methodology will provide the best sustained impact.

## Reference

1. http://theleanstartup.com/principles

Made in the USA
Monee, IL
13 September 2026

62975070R00063